U THANT IN NEW YORK, 1961–1971

U Thant as Vice-President of the UN General Assembly with Secretary-General Dag Hammarskjöld, September 1959.

RAMSES NASSIF

U Thant in New York
1961-1971

A Portrait of
the Third UN Secretary-General

WITH A FOREWORD BY SIR BRIAN URQUHART

ST. MARTIN'S PRESS, NEW YORK

Scholarly and Reference Division,
St. Martin's Press, Inc.,
175 Fifth Avenue, New York, NY 10010
First published in the United States of America in 1988
Printed in England on long-life paper
ISBN 0-312-02117-8

Library of Congress Cataloging-in-Publication Data

Nassif, Ramses.
  U Thant in New York, 1961–1971.

  Includes index.
    1. United Nations.   2. Thant, U, 1909–1974.
3. United Nations. Secretary General.   I. Title.
JX1977.N275   1988   341.23′24′0924   88–11674
ISBN 0-312-02117-8

To Rosaleen, Nabil and Nadine

ACKNOWLEDGEMENTS

I am deeply indebted to Sir Brian Urquhart, former UN Under Secretary-General, for agreeing to write a foreword to this book. Sir Brian, one of the pillars of the UN Secretariat, worked closely with U Thant on peace-keeping in the Middle East and Cyprus, and accompanied him on his crucial mission to Pakistan and India in 1965. His recently published autobiography, *A Life in Peace and War* (New York: Harper and Row, 1987), is fascinating, and a book which I highly recommend to students of history and international affairs.

I also acknowledge with gratitude the kindness of the late Dr Frederick Boland, President of the UN General Assembly in 1960–1 and later Chancellor of Trinity College, Dublin, who gave me generously of his time, and disclosed the inside story of how U Thant became a leading candidate for the post of Secretary-General in 1961, following the death of Dag Hammarskjöld.

To Rudolph Stadjuhar, spokesman for the Secretary-General, 1974–81, who helped me to obtain unrestricted access to the U Thant confidential papers in the UN Archives, New York; to A.M.E. Erlandsson, chief of the Archives Section and his colleagues; and to Mrs Lou Villacin of the UN press services, for their fine assistance to my research in New York, I also owe a great debt of gratitude.

Finally, I owe much to Mrs Barbara Stewart, Publisher of the *United Nations Observer and International Report*, New York, for her constant support, and to Miss Sheila Harden, Director of the David Davies Memorial Institute of International Studies, London, for invaluable advice on the final form of this book.

Geneva, February 1988   R.N.

v

FOREWORD

by Sir Brian Urquhart

This book about the third Secretary-General of the United Nations, U Thant, is a welcome event. U Thant was a public servant of outstanding courage and integrity, who served the world organisation for ten years with a quiet determination and distinction which have been all too little noted or remembered.

U Thant took over the office of Secretary-General after the tragic death of Dag Hammarskjöld, at a time of great stress and tension in the world organisation. By his calm and wise leadership he led the organisation away from a period of violent discord and confrontation and also presided over its fortunes at a time when the membership and thrust of the organisation were undergoing radical change and expansion. In a series of critical situations U Thant used his limited constitutional authority to the utmost to pre-empt or to curtail disaster. In the Cuban Missile Crisis, in his efforts to put an end to the Vietnam War, in his mission to India and Pakistan during the war of 1965, and on many other occasions he made a bold and single-minded attempt to restore or to preserve peace.

U Thant proved a useful scapegoat for the Middle East War of 1967, but it is less often recalled that he was the only world statesman who went to Cairo before that war to reason with President Nasser. (Ramses Nassif's account of this visit is of particular interest.) U Thant also proposed a number of measures by which the war might still have been prevented. When his efforts failed, he was shamelessly blamed for an international catastrophe which was largely the product of the uncontrolled and violent conflicting forces at work in the Middle East.

In this personal account of his association with U Thant as his press spokesman, Ramses Nassif has caught the very human and unusual quality of U Thant's personality – his strong sense of duty, the vital part that his Buddhist faith played in his life, his emphasis on morality and the importance of moral behaviour, his extraordinary lack of anger, resentment or envy, and his personal kindness and considerateness. I hope very much that this book will be the first step in a renewed effort to record for posterity the work of an outstanding servant of humanity.

NOTE ON STATEMENTS ATTRIBUTED TO U THANT

The reader may sometimes wonder who was the true author of the various statements and speeches of U Thant as UN Secretary-General which are quoted in this book – he himself or some anonymous speech-writer. The truth of the matter is that U Thant wrote many of them himself. On Cuba, Omar Loutfi and C.V. Narasimhan gave a helping hand – for obvious reasons, the Secretary-General did not involve Ralph Bunche or Brian Urquhart in this conflict. Statements, reports and speeches on the Middle East, the Congo and Cyprus were the exclusive domain of Bunche and Urquhart. U Thant himself drafted his statements on Czechoslovakia and the admission of Peking to the UN.

CONTENTS

PLATES

1

THE DEATH OF DAG HAMMARSKJÖLD AND THE APPOINTMENT OF U THANT

I first met U Thant in 1958 when he was Permanent Representative of Burma to the United Nations. We had a shared friend in Omar Loutfi, the Permanent Representative of Egypt. One of my assignments was as liaison officer with the Afro-Asian Group in the Office of Public Information of the UN Secretariat in New York. The Group had come into existence after the historic conference at Bandung (Indonesia) in 1955, and by 1958 it had gained prominence and recognition by sponsoring the cause of Algeria's independence. U Thant, Loutfi and Prince Ali Khan, the representative of Pakistan, were among the most prominent of the Group's ambassadors. In 1958, U Thant was chosen as Chairman of the Group's Standing Committee on Algeria, a unit set up to monitor developments in connection with this issue at the UN.

In 1960, the Congo crisis was looming over the United Nations. On June 23, the first central government was established with Joseph Kasavubu as President and Patrice Lumumba as Prime Minister; on June 30, the Republic of the Congo received its independence from Belgium; on July 5, the '*Force Publique*' mutinied in Leopoldville. This was a pretext for Belgian troops to intervene and occupy Leopoldville and Elisabethville. Confusion reigned. Moise Tshombe, President of the Katanga provincial government, proclaimed its secession on July 11. The following day, July 12, Lumumba requested the intervention of the United Nations in a cable addressed to Secretary-General Dag Hammarskjöld, who was attending the Economic and Social Council's summer session at Geneva. He cut short his stay there, flew back to New York and, for the first time, invoked article 99 of the UN Charter: 'The Secretary-General may bring to the attention of the Security Council any matter which, in his opinion, may threaten the maintenance of international peace and security.'

The Security Council appealed for a ceasefire and for the immediate withdrawal of Belgian troops, and authorised a UN Peacekeeping Force for the Congo. Hammarskjöld acted swiftly and boldly and, thanks to his initiative and drive, the Force was put together and despatched to the Congo. He also designated the American Ralph Bunche, Under

1

Secretary-General, who had gone to Leopoldville to represent the UN at the Congo's independence celebrations, as special representative. Bunche did not see eye to eye with Lumumba, and they clashed. The Soviet Union was not happy with Hammarskjöld's interpretation of the Security Council's resolutions, and suspected that he was working to promote United States interests in the Congo.

In addition to the Congo crisis, the situation in Berlin was getting worse. The Paris Summit between President Dwight Eisenhower and Chairman Nikita Khrushchev in May 1960 broke up in failure over the U2 incident (a United States spy plane had been shot down over the Soviet Union).

Against this background, Moscow declared that Khrushchev would lead the Soviet Delegation to the fifteenth session of the UN General Assembly in September. Every East European capital followed by announcing that its head of government would also attend. The momentum to come to New York grew, spurred by the fact that thirteen new African countries and Cyprus were to be admitted in September as members of the UN.

In addition to Khrushchev and the leaders of Eastern Europe, the 1960 Assembly was attended by Nehru of India, Nasser of Egypt, Nkrumah of Ghana, Sukarno of Indonesia and Sekou Toure of Guinea. President Eisenhower of the United States, the British Prime Minister Harold Macmillan, President Tito of Yugoslavia, King Hussein of Jordan and President Castro of Cuba were also there. Every movement those leaders made with their entourages in the corridors of the UN building was an event to be watched and filmed – prompting Thomas Hamilton, the brilliant but cynical correspondent of the *New York Times*, to label the 1960 General Assembly 'The Greatest Show on Earth'.

A great show or not, it was an exceptional gathering of world leaders that attended the opening of the Assembly on the afternoon of September 20, 1960. This was the same General Assembly that heard Khrushchev's speech, in plenary, calling for a *troika* to head the UN and thus replace its Secretary-General, who, he demanded, should immediately resign his post. Hammarskjöld, in a short and dignified address, retorted that he would stay on as long as the small nations who needed the protection of the United Nations wanted him to stay. His speech was received with a standing ovation, tremendous applause and shouts of 'Hear, Hear!'

A few days later, also in plenary, there was a procedural discussion regarding an item on colonialism that appeared on the provisional agenda. The discussion centred on whether it should be debated in plenary or be referred to the First Committee of the General Assembly. In the course of this debate, Khrushchev, Chairman of the Council of Ministers of the Soviet Union and General Secretary of its Communist Party, took his shoe in hand to pound the table in front of him. This incredible scene took place in full view of a few thousand people in the crowded Assembly hall and millions of TV-watchers around the world. At this point, the President of the Assembly, Frederick Boland of Ireland, livid with anger, struck his gavel and adjourned the meeting. The gavel broke in two pieces.

In September 1960, U Thant was Chairman of the Afro-Asian Group (the chairmanship rotated monthly among its members). He wanted to benefit from the presence of so many leaders at the UN and arranged for a meeting to exchange views. Aware of the importance of such a gathering, he was anxious to have Conference Room 4 as a venue. It was the largest room, reserved for the Political Committee as well as for the formal press conferences of the Secretary-General.

U Thant's secretary at the Burmese Mission called the meeting services department of the Secretariat, only to be told that Room 4 was out of the question, but that another room would be available. U Thant was upset and went into the delegates' North Lounge to confer with his colleagues. I happened to be passing, and he called me over to relate his dilemma over the venue for the meeting. I suggested that he personally telephone Hammarskjöld. Hammarskjöld readily complied with the wish of U Thant by arranging to shift the Political Committee elsewhere; Room 4 was set aside for the Afro-Asian meeting.

U Thant asked me to alert UN correspondents for a press briefing in 226, the press briefing room, at UN Headquarters. I advised that the briefing might well take place in Room 4, after the conclusion of the substantive meeting. This would guarantee a larger attendance, as well as TV coverage. He promptly agreed.

The briefing turned out to be well attended and was extensively covered. It was perhaps that single incident that influenced U Thant, a year later in November 1961, to choose me, from among half a dozen candidates, to be his spokesman and press officer when he was appointed Acting Secretary-General.

The following day, U Thant called on Hammarskjöld. During the conversation Hammarskjöld suggested that perhaps the Afro–Asian Group, with like-minded countries in Latin America, should adopt the name 'Third World'. 'After all,' he said, 'we already have the Old and the New Worlds, why not the Third World?' This was how a phrase which became part and parcel of UN terminology was coined.

At another meeting, as the two statesmen discussed development problems, U Thant complained that the poorer countries did not like being called 'underdeveloped', as they were referred to in the UN. Hammarskjöld interjected to say that he had been thinking about this, and had come up with the term 'developing' for the 'poor' countries, and 'developed' for the 'rich' ones. U Thant endorsed both terms and introduced them to members of his group. In recalling these anecdotes, he told me: 'Many people think I am the author of these original terms – I wish it were true!'

THE DEATH OF HAMMARSKJÖLD

The situation in the Congo deteriorated further, and with it the relations between Hammarskjöld and the Soviet Union. Andrew Cordier, the Secretary-General's Executive Assistant, another high official and an American, was sent to the Congo as Special Representative. It was a difficult period, which witnessed an open conflict between Kasavubu and Lumumba. During that time, Cordier ordered the national radio station to be closed, refusing Lumumba permission to broadcast against Kasavubu.

On September 12, Lumumba was arrested on the orders of Colonel Joseph Mobutu, Commander of the Congolese army (now President of Zaire), but then released. A few days later, Lumumba, dismissed by Kasavubu, took refuge in the Ghanaian officers' mess in Leopoldville. To offset Soviet criticism, Hammarskjöld appointed Rajeshwar Dayal, Ambassador of India to Pakistan, as the UN's Special Representative in the Congo.

On November 30, Lumumba was arrested by forces loyal to Kasavubu and was mysteriously flown to Elisabethville, the capital of Katanga province. He remained in captivity for a while but suddenly, on February 12, 1961, he and two of his companions were killed during an 'attempted escape'.

The cry was out for Hammarskjöld's blood. The Soviet Union, which considered Lumumba its man in the Congo, together with a chorus from Eastern Europe, accused Hammarskjöld of 'complicity'. It was true that Dayal, as UN Representative at the scene, had been insufficiently forceful enough in protecting Lumumba, and too legalistic in interpreting his mandate. It was argued that he should have ordered

UN forces to put Lumumba under protective custody to keep him away from Tshombe's mercenaries. But it was too late. Lumumba, the charismatic leader who had himself requested UN intervention, was now a murder victim. The UN had done nothing to save him, and Hammarskjöld was to be blamed.

The rupture between the Soviets and the UN Secretary-General was now complete. With confusion in the Congo and the Soviets mounting their pressure against him, Hammarskjöld decided to make one last desperate attempt. He hoped to meet Tshombe and thus pave the way for national reconciliation in the Congo. He left New York on September 12, 1961.

It was 7 a.m. on Monday, September 18, 1961. I was asleep in my apartment in Manhattan when the phone rang. It was Pauline Fredrick, the UN Correspondent of NBC (National Broadcasting Corporation), a well-known radio and TV commentator, and an admirer of Hammarskjöld. She was in tears – 'Dag's plane crashed near Ndola, he is dead, they are all dead.' Stunned, I did not know what to do. I dressed and went to the UN building, on the East River.

The news had spread and Andrew Cordier was already at his desk. He had lost his position as Executive Assistant to the Secretary-General in a reorganisation of the top echelon effected by Hammarskjöld just before his departure for the Congo, and had been replaced by C.V. Narasimhan (India) as *Chef de Cabinet*. Cordier had offered to resign, but was asked to stay on for a while in charge of General Assembly affairs, and continued to occupy the same office, next to the offices of the Secretary-General on the 38th floor. He remained my point of reference regarding guidance to the press, in my capacity as assistant to the UN spokesman, George Ivan Smith. Since he was away from New York, I went directly to see Cordier, and recommended a press conference the same morning. A few details of the tragedy had been received. Hammarskjöld had been accompanied by Hans Wieschhoff, an expert on African affairs, and Bill Ranallo, his Personal Assistant and bodyguard. The plane, called the *Albertina*, was a DC-6B, with a Swedish crew, from the UN Force in the Congo. It had taken off from Ndjili Airport at 4.51 p.m., local time (3.51 GMT), on September 17, on its way to Ndola (Northern Rhodesia) for a scheduled meeting with Tshombe. The *Albertina* crashed between 10.11 and 10.30 p.m. (GMT) on September 17, 1961.*

Cordier agreed there should be a press conference. The problem was who should conduct it. He could not undertake this task, nor could

---

* Brian Urquhart, *Hammarskjöld* (London and New York, 1972), pp. 588–9.

Ralph Bunche, the other senior American on Hammarskjöld's staff, since the Soviet Under Secretary-General, Georgi P. Arkadev, might make a public protest and mar what we wanted to be a solemn occasion, announcing the death of the Secretary-General of the UN. I suggested Tavares de Sa (Brazil), the head of the Office of Public Information; Cordier endorsed the idea and called Tavares to alert him.

The press was there in force. Tavares de Sa read a statement giving the facts of the crash. There were dozens of questions: How did it happen? Was there an explosion on board? What would happen to the UN Secretariat? Who would direct it? There were no immediate answers, and the large number of correspondents filtered out of Conference Room 4 to write speculative stories about the power-struggle within the Secretariat and the candidates for the post of Secretary-General.

Before Hammarskjöld's death, there was a non-aligned conference of Heads of State in Belgrade on September 1–6, 1961. U Thant had participated as a member of the Burmese delegation, headed by Premier U Nu; it was an opportunity for him to renew his contacts with the leaders he had come to know during the 1960 General Assembly in New York.

With Hammarskjöld gone, Khrushchev's *troika* proposal, made a year earlier, was revived. He had insisted that the Secretary-General be replaced by three: one representing the Eastern Bloc, one for the West and one for the Group of non-aligned countries. But the call for a *troika* had little support. Premier Nehru's statement on September 18 paid tribute to Hammarskjöld's efforts in the Congo, and carefully ignored the *troika* proposal. President Kennedy issued a statement in Washington rejecting the *troika* and reiterating US support for a single Secretary-General.

On September 19, 1961, the UN General Assembly opened in New York and elected Mongi Slim of Tunisia as President to succeed Boland of Ireland. Press speculation was rife. Mongi Slim, Frederick Boland and Ralph Enckell of Finland were mentioned as possible candidates for the post of Secretary-General.

IRELAND'S ROLE IN THE NEW APPOINTMENT

On May 19, 1981, while reminiscing at his home in Dublin about those days twenty years earlier, Dr Frederick Boland told me that Ambassador Valery Zorin, the Soviet representative to the UN, had asked him if he was interested in the post of Secretary-General. Boland's reply was 'No thank you, I have had a full year as President of the Assembly and that is more than I can take.'

On October 2, 1961, Boland called on Andrei Gromyko, the Foreign Minister at the Soviet UN Mission on Park Avenue. Boland had established a reputation with the Soviets since he broke the gavel, and they treated him with respect; he invited U Thant to go along with him as Chairman of the Afro–Asian Group. U Thant was unaware that Boland had reached the conclusion that he would be a candidate whom the Soviets could not veto.

The discussion with Gromyko centred on the *troika* – its impracticality and the need to preserve the principle of the UN Charter that there should be one Secretary-General. An hour later, as they left Gromyko, they took with them the impression that the Soviets would not insist on the *troika*, or veto a candidate from the Afro–Asian Group, but that to save face they would demand that the Secretary-General appoint a group of principal advisers, including one from the Soviet Union to assist him in discharging his duties.

Boland reported his impressions to Adlai Stevenson of the United States and members of the Western Group. A subsequent rumour that a plan was afoot to draft Mongi Slim of Tunisia as Secretary-General *ad interim* boosted U Thant's chances. The Israelis were adamant against having an Arab in the post; the United States too was not enthusiastic, and the Soviet Union considered Slim pro-Western.

The Arabs as a whole, while suspicious of Burma's links with Israel, were nevertheless appreciative of U Thant's efforts on behalf of Algeria. The moderation and far-sightedness of two of their ambassadors, Omar Loutfi of Egypt and Adnan Pachachi of Iraq, were instrumental in securing the support of the Arab Bloc. It was a unique situation where a diplomat from a small Buddhist country in Asia had the support of both Arabs and Israelis.

U Thant's close friendship to U Nu was an asset. Rangoon's ambassadors were lobbying for him, and President Kwame Nkrumah of Ghana went as far as suggesting to Nehru, Tito, Nasser and Sukarno that the non-aligned should take the initiative in proposing a suitable candidate from a small Asian country, to be assisted by three deputies (East, West and Afro–Asian).

The United States and Britain, anxious to break the deadlock, said that they would by-pass the Security Council, to avoid the Soviet veto, and go directly to the General Assembly. The Soviets immediately responded by declaring the move illegal under the UN Charter. For weeks, there evolved what was termed the numbers game. One Secretary-General with five advisers (US, Soviet, West European, African, and Latin American) was a proposal favoured by Adlai Stevenson, while Zorin advocated seven advisers, adding Eastern Europe and Asia.

Armand Bérard, the French Ambassador to the UN, was a close friend of U Thant and helped influence Paris to go along with the rest of Western Europe. His country had their reservations because U Thant did not know French, the language of diplomacy, which Hammarskjöld spoke fluently. Then there was a silly rumour that a French 'source' called U Thant 'too short'! When he heard these rumblings, the quiet, self-composed diplomat made his undiplomatic comment when chatting with Bill Oatis of the Associated Press: 'Bill, you can tell them that I am taller than Napoleon, who did not speak English!'

The numbers game persisted and the press corps accredited to the UN were impatient – there was much speculation and little hard news. They approached U Thant to be the guest of UNCA (UN Correspondents Association) at their monthly luncheon, an event which usually turned into a press conference after a hurried meal. He hesitated, fearing that anything he said might upset his chances. I added my voice to those of the correspondents, arguing that it was time he spoke up and gave his views. He finally accepted.

At the luncheon, which took place at Danny's Hideaway, a favourite steakhouse for journalists and radio commentators, a few blocks from the UN building, he declared that he would come up with his own formula regarding the number of advisers, in the hope of breaking the deadlock. That was October 26, 1961.

On October 29, U Thant agreed to appear on a TV programme with Stevenson. Answering a question from the moderator, he said: 'Whoever occupies the office of the Secretary-General of the United Nations must be impartial but not necessarily neutral' – adding: 'In regard to moral issues, he could not and should not remain neutral or passive.' In the years that followed, U Thant lived up to those words.

Suddenly, there was a thaw in the numbers game. The United States and Britain said that they would leave the final decision in the hands of the new Secretary-General. Ambassador Zorin reluctantly went along with this, and the stage was set for the appointment of U Thant.

The Security Council – which, according to the Charter, must elect the Secretary-General – met at 11 a.m. on November 3, 1961. Ambassador Omar Loutfi of Egypt was President of the Council, which met *in camera* – only delegates and interpreters were allowed to be present. The Council adjourned shortly after one o'clock, and I waited with the correspondents to hear what the President of the Council would say.

He told us that a communiqué would be issued within minutes giving the result of the Council's deliberations. With that he left, and I followed. Before I spoke, Loutfi said: 'It is our friend U Thant – unanimous decision.' I immediately went looking for U Thant to give him the news. I found him in the North Lounge talking to members of his delegation. 'Congratulations are in order,' I said breathlessly and we shook hands. He answered with a smile, saying 'I hope your source is a good one!'

That same afternoon the General Assembly met and appointed U Thant Acting Secretary-General to serve the unexpired term of Dag Hammarskjöld till April 1963. In his acceptance speech, U Thant stated that it was his intention to invite a limited number of persons to act as his principal Advisers, among them Georgi Arkadev from the Soviet Union and Ralph Bunche from the United States.

Thus the quiet Burmese diplomat was appointed to what Trygve Lie, the first Secretary-General of the UN, described as 'the most impossible job on earth'. U Thant was fifty-two years old.

2

THE MODEST DIPLOMAT FROM BURMA

U Thant came from a modest background. He was born at Pantanaw, Burma, on January 22, 1909, the son of a prosperous rice miller, and educated at the National High School in Pantanaw and at University College, Rangoon. At the age of twenty, he won the All-Burma Translation Competition organised by the Education Association. He entered the world of diplomacy as a teacher, newspaperman and civil servant. He served as Senior Master of the National High School and became Headmaster after winning first place in a teachers' examination. He was also active as a free-lance journalist.

During his diplomatic career, U Thant served on several occasions as Adviser to Prime Ministers U Nu and U Ba Swe. From 1956 to 1961, he was Permanent Representative of Burma to the UN. During that period, he headed the Burmese delegations to four sessions of the General Assembly, and in 1959 he was one of the Vice-Presidents of the Assembly's fourteenth session. In 1961, before his appointment as Acting Secretary-General, he was Chairman of the United Nations Congo Conciliation Commission.

When the congratulations on his appointment were over, I sought him out to check his biography. I explained that I had received a copy from the Burmese Mission, and advised him to go over it carefully since the Office of Public Information would print it as the official biography of the new Secretary-General – or 'SG' as he was referred to in the Secretariat. We went together to a small conference room in the vicinity of the Security Council chamber. He sat at a desk, pulled a Parker fountain-pen from his pocket, and went over each word and punctuation mark like the schoolteacher he had been.

He came across a sentence about his visit to Israel with Prime Minister U Nu. He stopped and, looking straight into my eyes, said: 'What do you think? The Arabs were friendly to me; so were the Israelis who, as you know, have close relations with Burma. Should I leave it or should I rephrase it?' I did not respond. I was not prepared to give advice so early in the game and on such a delicate subject. Finally he observed my hesitation and, answering his own question, said: 'Perhaps it would be wiser to eliminate the names of all countries visited.'

He crossed them out and put instead – 'U Thant also accompanied U Nu as adviser on visits to several countries in Asia and Europe.' When he finished reviewing and approving the biography, I cut out that paragraph, wrote it out in my handwriting and gave it back to him to initial.

He appreciated this gesture and said with a smile: 'Thank you for being so thoughtful.' I had a feeling that the man was either testing me or hinting, in his discreet oriental way, that he was beginning to trust me. Whatever it was, I found myself saying, 'This will remain confidential.' And it did. For I never mentioned this matter or discussed it with anyone until the writing of these pages.

On November 4, 1961, his first day in office as Secretary-General, I was by chance his first appointment. I thought I should wait for him with the correspondents in the lobby of the UN Secretariat. When he arrived in his chauffeur-driven black Cadillac, he stopped to chat with them and then asked me to accompany him in the elevator.

A Dutch woman who had been Hammarskjöld's secretary for several years was at her customary desk in the outer office. Always conscious of her importance as the person closest to the SG on the thirty-eighth floor of the glass house, she snapped 'Have you an appointment?' I said: 'Yes, the SG asked me to come.'

U Thant kept me for over an hour talking about the press, the correspondents he knew, his plans for them. He wanted to give a series of luncheons in his private dining-room on the thirty-eighth floor for about ten or twelve journalists at a time. He asked if there was a precedent for such functions. I said there was none and added that Hammarskjöld had been reserved in his relations with the press.

I mentioned the importance of his first press conference and advised that he should give one as soon as possible. He then asked detailed questions as to who organised the Secretary-General's press conferences, how often they were held and who attended them from the UN Secretariat. Twice, Miss Platz came in to say that C.V. Narasimhan, the *Chef de Cabinet*, and two other aides were waiting to see him. He said 'Yes, yes', an expression that we came to learn meant 'I know and I don't want to hear about it any more!' Before I left, he asked if I would like to be his press officer, and I replied that it would be a great privilege and honour. He smiled and said nothing.

At his first press conference on December 1, 1961, his opening remarks were: 'Ladies and Gentlemen of the Fourth Estate, I am very glad indeed that I have at last had an opportunity to meet with you. In view of my own background, no one could be more conscious of the need for keeping all of you informed of the manifold activities of the United Nations, and by that I mean not exclusively the work of the Secretariat.

'The United Nations is an organisation whose strength depends upon the support it gets from enlightened public opinion all over the world, and you are in the best position to make it possible for that opinion to be not only enlightened, but also well informed.'

He continued: 'I know it has been a tradition of the House that the Secretary-General does not hold a press conference while the General Assembly is in session. However, I felt that I should have this meeting with you even while the Assembly was in session because I have not had a chance to meet with you since my election as Acting Secretary-General. I would also hope that once the Assembly had completed its work, we might meet more regularly.'

In the years to come he kept that promise, and throughout his ten-year administration the number of formal press conferences and briefings he held exceeded 100.

For U Thant the press conference was a pleasant experience. He had a natural warmth towards journalists and was comfortable with them. While he was Ambassador of Burma, long before becoming Secretary-General, he had made it a practice to drop in on friends in the press area, on the third floor of the Secretariat building. He enjoyed thinking of himself as a former journalist, and often mentioned this. He was keenly aware that an enlightened information programme was essential for the success of the United Nations.

A few days after his first press conference, he received a complaint from the United Nations Correspondents Association (UNCA). They had wanted to check a question relating to the Security Council after 6.00 p.m. but had not been able to do so because everyone in the Office of Public Information had gone home. That was a Friday afternoon. He summoned me to his office to show me the letter and told me he was calling a meeting in his conference room for 10.30 a.m. the following day, a Saturday. He asked me to alert the chiefs of press services and the Head of OPI to be there. When I said that perhaps it would be better for his office to call them, because I knew they hated to break their week-end and most of them never saw the building on a Saturday morning, he simply said 'No – I want you to do it.' I did so, of course, thus making myself unpopular with the powers that be in OPI. To those who protested and questioned my request, I said I was carrying out the instructions of the SG. To those who asked 'Why You?', I answered

'Ask the Secretary-General' and hung up. I was young and bold and felt that the Secretary-General would protect me.

The meeting took place and all the chiefs were there. When we were assembled, he read from notes he himself had prepared. He declared that as of Monday there would be a daily briefing at 12 noon to be given by Osgood Carruthers, an American journalist who had been recruited by Hammarskjöld to act as United Nations spokesman, and Ramses Nassif, 'my press officer'. It was the first time he referred to me in those terms. I was proud but scared. Looking at the surprised faces of the chiefs around me, I thought, 'they outrank me in grade, age and experience – may God help me in carrying out this difficult and delicate task.'

Tavares de Sa, the Head of OPI, wanted to make a comment, but U Thant interrupted him to say 'I haven't finished', and continued to direct that a senior press officer must be on duty every working day until all meetings had adjourned and must check with the Secretary-General's Office before 'the lid is on', a phrase we coined in press services to mean that all was quiet and correspondents could go home. U Thant recalled his remarks at the press conference a few days earlier, that he considered the representatives of the information media 'members of the Fourth Estate', and reiterated the importance he attached to them and the essential role they played in publicising the work of the UN. He added that he would issue instructions on Monday to all heads of departments and programmes to come to the daily briefings from time to time, and to give out to the press as much news and information as possible. He then concluded with these words: 'Thank you very much, the meeting is over.'

He handled that meeting in an abrupt way, unlike the gentle and polite man he was. I found out later that it was a deliberate attempt on his part to establish, early in his administration, that politeness should not be misconstrued as weakness, and that he knew as much as the experts about press matters and public opinion.

The press briefings at noon, every day from Monday to Friday, were inaugurated the following Monday and have since become a part of life at UN Headquarters.

Throughout his ten-year tenure, he often employed blunt words in answering correspondents' questions. At his first press conference on December 1, 1961, replying to a question on the Congo he said 'Tshombe [the Katangan leader] is a very unstable man.'

At a press conference in Ottawa on May 26, 1964, he was asked to comment on a suggestion that atomic bombs should be used in Vietnam (Senator Barry Goldwater had made this statement, and the item was carried in the *New York Times*). U Thant replied, 'As you are no doubt aware, I am against the use of atomic weapons for destructive purposes anywhere, under any circumstances. Anybody who proposes the use of atomic weapons is, in my view, out of his mind.'

Paul Martin, the prominent Canadian Minister for External Affairs and U Thant's host on this occasion, was sitting next to him. The moment U Thant finished his sentence, Martin pounded the table and shouted 'Hear, Hear'.

Encouraged by Paul Martin's enthusiasm, U Thant continued 'Let me elaborate there is, in my view a racial factor in such a projected operation . . . In 1945, when atomic bombs were dropped over Hiroshima and Nagasaki in Japan, there was a widespread feeling in many parts of Asia that these deadly atomic weapons were dropped on Japanese cities because the Japanese were non-whites, and it was also argued at that time that atomic bombs would never have been dropped over cities in Nazi Germany, which was also at war with the Allies. So there is a racial element which I would commend to the attention of those who are thinking of launching such atomic blasts.'

These remarks made front-page headlines in the Canadian and American press. I expected a savage reaction, blasting U Thant, from Senator Goldwater, known for his bluntness and his dislike of the United Nations. But none came.

On October 22, 1964, at a press conference at UN Headquarters in New York, U Thant was asked to comment on 'Mr Khrushchev's displacement and the method used'. He answered: 'Well, it is not proper, of course, in my position to make an assessment of a situation like the one which we witnessed in the Soviet Union last week since they are primarily domestic matters. But if I may venture an opinion, after the change of leadership in the Soviet Union I do not think the government will pursue a foreign policy different from the one adopted by Mr Khrushchev.'

He continued: 'Actually, last Friday Mr Federenko [the Soviet Ambassador to the UN] informed me of the change in the Soviet leadership and transmitted the line of the new government – that it would continue to pursue the policies of peaceful coexistence, disarmament and the peaceful settlement of international disputes and strengthening of the United Nations.

'Incidentally, I happen to have known Mr Brezhnev since 1955. I met him in Alma Ata at the time when he was head of the Communist Party of Kazakhstan. I met him again in 1962 in Moscow, and again last year on the occasion of the signing in Moscow of the partial nuclear test ban treaty. I found him the same friendly, warm and unaffected gentleman with a deep knowledge of world affairs. I also knew Mr Kosygin. I met him several times – he is one of the most respected leaders of the Soviet Union.

'As regards Mr Khrushchev, I have made my assessment of him on several occasions. I still believe that he will be long remembered as a man who tried his best to implement the principle of peaceful coexistence – and he did that with some degree of success in that he had been able to convince a considerable segment of public opinion in the West of his sincerity.'

At this point U Thant paused and added in a clear crisp voice: 'I think it would be helpful, and even desirable, if Mr Khrushchev were able, or inclined, to make a public statement on the circumstances leading to his exit.' The words fell like a bombshell on the assembled journalists who had packed Conference Room 4. There was silence and the only sound you could hear was the shuffle of paper. These remarks were front-page headlines in the *New York Times* and other newspapers around the world the following day. When I checked with the TASS (Soviet News Agency) Bureau at the UN on whether they were using U Thant's statement, I was told curtly: 'Yes, we are telexing everything verbatim.' A few weeks later, I found out, from the UN Information Centre in Moscow, that both *Pravda* and *Izvestia*, the two leading Moscow dailies had indeed carried the statement while omitting all references to Khrushchev.

U Thant served as Acting Secretary-General from November 1961, when he was unanimously appointed by the General Assembly on the recommendation of the Security Council to fill the unexpired term of the late Dag Hammarskjöld, till November 30, 1962, when he was, again unanimously, appointed Secretary-General for a term of office ending on November 3, 1966. On 2 December, 1966, he was unanimously reappointed – for a second term. He retired on December 31, 1971.

THE ROLE OF THE SECRETARY-GENERAL

U Thant had strong views on the role of the Secretary-General. In an address at a luncheon for the Dag Hammerskjöld Memorial Scholarship Fund of the United Nations Correspondents Association (UNCA) on September 16, 1971, he defined that role in detail. He said, 'Every

Secretary-General brings to the Office his own personality, ideas and methods. The efforts and experiences, achievements and failures, of successive Secretaries-General are the raw materials out of which the Office has developed over the years on the basis of the very general description which is given in the Charter. Each Secretary-General must build, as best he can, on the Office as he inherited it. If he cannot hope to repeat all the successes of his predecessors, neither should he fear to try again where they failed.

'No Secretary-General can afford to lose a sense of obligation to the human community in its broadest sense . . . while it is debatable whether the Secretary-General is – or should try to be – the conscience of mankind, he must certainly never lose a strong personal sense of justice, of humanity, and of the importance of human dignity.

'The other quality which a Secretary-General can never afford to lose is an urgent sense of political realism. The Secretary-General operates under the Charter in a world of independent sovereign states, where national interests remain dominant despite ideological, technological and scientific changes, and despite the obvious dangers of unbridled national-ism. He works within the paradox that as these sovereign states in fact become increasingly interdependent, the forces of nationalism often lead them to assert more and more stridently their rivalries with each other . . .

'There is a persistent illusion that the Secretary-General's position is in some way comparable to that of the head of a government, and that clear-cut and decisive action can and should be taken by him on problems which have defied the collective wisdom of the 127 member-governments. The truth, of course, is that the United Nations and the Secretary-General have none of the attributes of sovereignty, and no independent power, although the Secretary-General has, and must maintain, his independence of judgement, and must never become the agent of any particular gov-ernment or group of governments.

'No parliament enacts for the Secretary-General the detailed and enforceable legislation that provides a Prime Minister with precise and continuous directives. No clear-cut policy illuminates his course of action. He is supported by none of the great permanent establishments of a state, and lacks the first-hand sources of information upon which governments can base their plans.

'More often than not, he faces the conflicts of the present or the problems of the future with vague or non-existent directives, with an exiguous budget and, in the case of some peacekeeping operations or of vast relief problems, with resources based solely on voluntary contributions. These are some of the limitations of the Secretary-Generalship.

'I feel strongly that the Secretary-General, irrespective of his personal views on any issue, is obliged to stand by every resolution or decision of the main deliberative organs of the United Nations. . . . The Secretary-General has no option whatsoever in this regard, whatever may be the temporary effect on his relations with individual member-states. Nor can he seek an escape from a resolution of an organ of the United Nations because it may appear to be unpractical or even unfair . . .

'It is Article 99 of the Charter that gives the Secretary-General explicit political responsibility in his own right. The Preparatory Commission of the United Nations elaborated on Article 99 in its report as follows: "The Secretary-General may have an important role to play as a mediator and as an informal adviser of many governments, and will undoubtedly be called upon from time to time, in the exercise of his administrative duties, to take decisions which may justly be called political." Under Article 99 of the Charter, moreover, he has been given a quite special right which goes beyond any power previously accorded to the head of an international organisation, viz. to bring to the attention of the Security Council any matter (not merely any dispute or situation) which, in his opinion, may threaten the maintenance of international peace and security. It is impossible to foresee how this Article will be applied: but the responsibility it confers upon the Secretary-General will require the exercise of the highest qualities of political judgement, tact and integrity.'

Early in his administration, U Thant realised the lack of interest of the information media in the social and economic activities of the United Nations, and repeatedly complained that in spite of the fact that over 80 per cent of the staff of the UN family worked in the economic and social fields, the information media were only interested in highlighting the political developments in the Security Council and the General Assembly. To help correct the situation, he gave his full support to the creation of the Centre for Economic and Social Information. It started as a small unit and gradually grew into a large and important division in the OPI (Office of Public Information).

THE ECONOMIC DIMENSION

Coming from Burma, a poor developing country in Asia, he was keenly aware of the problems of development. President John F. Kennedy had addressed the General Assembly on September 25, 1961 suggesting that there should be a concerted programme of action in the fields of economic and social development. That was the origin of the idea of the 'First Development Decade'.

On December 19, 1961, six weeks after U Thant became Acting Secretary-General, the Assembly unanimously endorsed the suggestion and requested that he develop proposals for the intensification of action in the fields of economic and social development, and present them to the Economic and Social Council (ECOSOC) at its 34th session (the summer of 1962).

Armed with this mandate from the General Assembly, the gap between the rich and poor countries, the North and South, became one of his favourite themes. In a statement at a press conference devoted to plans for the UN Development Decade, at New York, on June 14, 1962, he stated: 'In the decade of the 1950s the rate of economic progress of at least one third of the human race – the poorest third who are intent on conquering their own poverty – was dangerously slow. But in the same period the economies of the highly developed countries, starting from a very much higher base, have been growing faster. And thus the already huge gap between their living standards and those of the less developed nations has widened still further. These material facts are dangerously in conflict with a psychological or spiritual fact: namely, that the peoples themselves who are victims of this situation, and still more their leaders, nowadays look upon the perpetration of poverty in a world of plenty as morally wrong and politically intolerable. Most of them have only recently achieved sovereign independence, and they are determined to use their new political liberty to escape from the bondage of want. From this state of affairs arise pressures for change which may build up to dangerous and explosive levels unless they can find a constructive outlet.'

The report requested by the General Assembly in December 1961 was completed in six months. This was a gigantic achievement made possible by the dedicated efforts of Philippe de Seynes, a resourceful French economist who was the head of the Department of Economic and Social Affairs of the UN Secretariat, and his able colleagues. U Thant flew to Geneva and presented the report personally to ECOSOC, in a major speech, on July 9, 1962, opening the debate on the subject.

He based his proposals for action on his belief that the psychological climate was favourable for a concerted attack on the problems of under-development and his conviction that the United Nations, despite its modest resources, was a good vehicle for focusing international attention on these problems. U Thant proposed a number of priority objectives to help developing countries formulate sound development plans. They included mobilising national resources, technical assistance in vocational education and technical training, food production, trade, housing, health, transport, communications, science and technology. Unfortunately, many of these objectives were not attained.

Again, in an address before ECOSOC in Geneva on July 16, 1964, he said: 'I have often said, and I feel it bears repetition, that North–South tensions are fundamentally as serious as East-West ones and that the United Nations has a unique contribution to make towards the lessening of both . . . I would like to express here the belief that today the world economic situation is characterised by increased determination on the part of the developing countries to plead their case, greater willingness on the part of the industrialised ones to listen to the plea, and, as a result, by a better chance for a proper understanding all around of the problems involved and their inter-relations.'

U Thant's remarks uttered in 1962 and 1964 bear repetition today, for little has improved in the area of North–South relations.

U Thant worked tirelessly for the establishment of the United Nations Conference on Trade and Development (UNCTAD). In a speech in December 1964, he declared: 'The year 1964 has witnessed the deliberations of the United Nations Conference on Trade and Development, the largest intergovernmental conference ever assembled, with representatives of 119 states participating in it. This conference has already been recognised as an event of historic importance likely to have a significant impact on international cooperation for decades to come. The Final Act of the Conference represents the culmination of efforts and discussions over almost two decades, during which new political forces and ideas of international cooperation were gradually taking shape within the United Nations.'

When the time came to appoint the first Secretary-General of UNCTAD, U Thant was impressed by Raul Prebisch, a prominent economist from Argentina, who had the full support of the Latin American Group at the UN. When word leaked out about this, U Thant was told that the Americans were not enthusiastic about Prebisch, for they considered him too liberal, and the Arabs were unhappy because it was rumoured that he was 'pro-Israel'. At this point, U Thant said: 'The Secretary-General is always damned if he does and damned if he does not – I think Prebisch is the best man for the job.' He appointed Raul Prebisch as Secretary-General of UNCTAD and the General Assembly took note of the appointment without discussion.

A GOOD BUDDHIST

U Thant was kind and tolerant. He wrote: 'I was trained to be tolerant of everything except intolerance. I was brought up not only to develop the spirit of tolerance, but also to cherish moral and spiritual qualities, especially modesty, humility, compassion and, most important, to attain a certain degree of emotional equilibrium. I was taught to control my emotions through a process of concentration and meditation. Of course, being human, and not yet having reached the stage of Arahant or Arhat (one who attains perfect enlightenment), I cannot completely control my emotions, but I must say that I am not easily excited or excitable.'

His love for children knew no bounds. In his ten years as Secretary-General, he rarely missed a function in support of UNICEF, for there were always children present at those receptions. He enjoyed meeting and talking to them, and UNICEF helped deprived children throughout the world.

In July 1963, while on an official visit to Bulgaria, he was invited to have lunch at a cooperative farm outside the capital, Sofia. The managers of the farm and the leaders of the community had gathered at the Mayor's house to greet their important guest. A pretty five-year-old girl in a white dress stood there, carrying a bouquet of roses. The manager of the farm whispered proudly. 'She has a nice speech in English.' The girl approached U Thant, gave him the flowers with a smile and then suddenly burst into tears. 'I forget my speech!' she cried. Protocol went out of the window. U Thant ignored the schedule and everybody else. He took the little girl in his arms and said softly, 'I don't like speeches anyway. I came here to meet you . . . please don't cry, and give me a smile.' She did – and the ceremony and the luncheon took place as scheduled.

In his private life, U Thant was rather lonely. His wife Daw Thien Tin never learned English and rarely attended UN functions. When he had to entertain official couples, his daughter Aye Aye, a stunning petite woman who loved beautiful clothes, acted as his hostess.

U Thant lost his only son Tin Maung in tragic circumstances. It was on 21 May, 1962, at about 11.40 in the morning, that the phone rang in my office. It was Bruce Munn, Chief of the UPI Bureau at the UN. 'Ramses, we have a bulletin from Rangoon that U Thant's son Tin Maung was killed in an accident. I will keep this item off the wire until you have had a chance to tell him.'

It was common knowledge that U Thant listened to the news on

WQXR (the *New York Times* radio station) practically every hour, on the hour, and Munn thoughtfully wanted to spare him the shock of hearing it suddenly on the radio. I put down the receiver and took the elevator to the thirty-eighth floor. When I reached his office I hesitated. I thought, why should I go alone to convey this sad news? I stopped at the office of Narasimhan, only to find he was at a meeting. I told his secretary that I needed to see him urgently, and asked her to get him out. This she did. I told him the news and asked if he would come along with me. When we entered the office, U Thant was fiddling with the squawk box which enabled him to listen to any meeting taking place in the building as well as the news. Something was wrong with one of the buttons and he said with a smile: 'Nothing works in the Secretary-General's office.' He noticed our grave faces and stopped. We gave him the news. His first reaction was 'I wonder how my wife will take it.' He was completely composed. His acceptance was part of a disciplined ability to keep his balance, which came with his Buddhist training.

As Acting Secretary-General, in 1962, U Thant made official visits to Sweden, Denmark and the United Kingdom. He also visited Norway, Switzerland, the Soviet Union (at the invitation of Chairman Khrushchev), Poland, Czechoslovakia, Austria – and Washington, at the invitation of President Kennedy.

The very first invitation came from the Government of Sweden, thanks to Mrs Agda Rossell, the Swedish Ambassador to the UN who was one of U Thant's admirers. In sounding him out, she said that he should make his first official visit as Secretary-General to Sweden, the country that had produced his eminent predecessor, Dag Hammarskjöld. U Thant readily accepted and agreed on a date. Two days later, an invitation followed from Denmark. He briefed me about his travel plans and asked me to prepare a press release to be issued at the noon briefing. After the briefing, I had a luncheon appointment with Robin Haydon, the spokesman for the British Mission to the UN (Sir Robin was British Ambassador to Ireland from 1976, until his retirement in 1980). In the course of our conversation, I told Haydon about the Swedish and Danish invitations and added: 'It would be wonderful if U Thant would also visit London.' He enthusiastically agreed; he felt that his boss, Sir Patrick Dean, the British Ambassador, would recommend it to Lord Home, the Foreign Secretary. Two hours after our luncheon, Robin Haydon telephoned to say that Sir Patrick was seeing U Thant to discuss plans for this visit with him.

A few days later, the invitation came through, and Britain was added to U Thant's itinerary. In the course of the visit, U Thant had a private audience with Queen Elizabeth II, on July 6, 1962. At Her Majesty's request, they were alone and she kept him for forty minutes. I was waiting with the rest of the entourage in one of the reception rooms when U Thant emerged from the royal audience. He took me aside to brief me on what should be included in my daily press cable to UN Headquarters in New York. Instead he started by saying 'Ramses, there is something I want you to know – the first thing the Queen said was, "As a mother I know how much you must have suffered when you heard the terrible news of the death of your son. I thought of you and I thought of your wife when the news was brought to my attention." He then said: 'There were tears in the Queen's eyes and there were tears in mine.' Needless to say, this was not part of my cable to New York, and I have kept this episode buried till today.

In February 1964, U Thant visited Algeria, Morocco and Tunisia. President Ben Bella, together with his entire Cabinet, was at the airport in Algiers to receive him. This was followed by inspection of a guard of honour and a 21-gun salute, honours reserved normally only for a head of state. It was the first time in the history of the UN that its Secretary-General had had such a reception. 'It was Algeria's way to say to U Thant – thank you for what you had done for our cause of independence, as Chairman of the Afro-Asian Committee on Algeria. . .' were Ben Bella's words, translated by an interpreter. The Algerian reception set a precedent, and several member-states of the UN elected to follow suit, by according the Secretary-General the status of a head of state. When Kurt Waldheim, the fourth Secretary-General (1972–82), visited Manila in May 1979 to open UNCTAD V, President Marcos was at the airport to greet him with full military honours and a 21-gun salute.

It was also during his visit to Algeria that U Thant was invited to address the National Assembly, the first foreign visitor to receive such an honour. He gave his address on February 4, 1964. The theme of his speech, delivered in English and simultaneously translated into French and Arabic, was 'Africa and the World Community'.

U Thant had strong feelings about the sanctity of the human person. In 1971, in the introduction to the *Report of the Secretary-General on the work of the Organisation* – his last – he said: 'I feel more strongly than ever that the worth of the individual human being is the most unique and precious of all our assets and must be the beginning and the end of all our efforts. Governments, systems, ideologies and institutions come and go, but humanity remains. The nature and value of this most precious asset is increasingly appreciated as we see how empty organised life becomes when we remove or suppress the infinite variety and vitality of the individual.'

His actions were dominated by a desire to identify the highest religious convictions with political morality. It was in this spirit that, in an address to the special meeting held in San Francisco in 1965 to mark the twentieth anniversary of the signing of the United Nations Charter, U Thant made a memorable statement. He said, 'On the occasion of the twentieth anniversary of the United Nations, I would like to express the following wishes for humanity: – I wish that men cease to hate and kill their fellow-men for reasons of race, colour, religion, nationalism or ideology;

'– I wish that more love, compassion and understanding guide the management of human affairs; – I wish that the rich and privileged share their blessings with the poor; – I wish that nations enrich each other in the art of governing men in peace, justice and prosperity;

'– I wish that all nations unite to face with courage and determination the unprecedented worldwide problems that lie in store for humanity; – I wish that the immense progress achieved in science and technology be equalled in the spheres of morality, justice and politics;

'– I wish that the world listen more attentively to the concerned voice of youth; – I wish that the leaders of the great nations of our time surmount their differences and unite their efforts for the benefits of all mankind.'

It was after his meeting with the Office of Public Information, at which he decided to start the daily press briefings, that U Thant introduced me to Josephine Blacklock, a handsome Australian woman in her forties, who for several years had been his private secretary at the Burmese Mission to the UN. He added: 'Mrs Blacklock will be your assistant in your capacity as my press officer – C.V. [Narasimhan] will explain her duties and will help you write her job description.'

It was a royal command. Josephine was installed in a small office next to mine on the third floor, in the press area. Narasimhan dutifully took care of the administrative action for her appointment in the Office of Public Information, and I handled the delicate task of explaining her presence, in the exposed press area, to the curious correspondents. To the few who mattered, I said that she was there to sort out the Secretary-General's private mail; also to clip articles from magazines and journals for his personal attention.

In his ten years as Secretary-General, U Thant saw Josephine in his office on every working day, from Monday to Friday, for about 30–45 minutes. It was always tête-à-tête, and no one interrupted. If there was an urgent message, Estella Mira, his private secretary, would knock, enter and hand him a note and walk out.

Josephine worshipped U Thant, and there was no doubt that he valued her friendship and enjoyed her company. To the queries I received from correspondents, at one time or another: 'What does she really do?', I maintained my silence. The subject did not go beyond that. There was never a single item written about U Thant and Josephine, a further testimony to the respect and affection that existed between him and the press corps at the UN.

Josephine's pleasant personality and discretion helped in this direction. Through her knowledge of reading the horoscope, she established friendships with several colleagues and reporters. Knowing her closeness to U Thant, I suspected that she must have read his horoscope. When I asked him privately whether he believed in the horoscope, he replied: 'I do not believe in it, nor do I reject it – but let me tell you, there are many great people in Asia who would not take a major decision without consulting their horoscope.'

Early in 1971, Josephine confided in me that she was concerned about U Thant's health. Later that year, he was rushed to hospital with a bleeding ulcer. When he had recovered, several weeks later, he was allowed to return to his office. Cancer was diagnosed soon after his retirement at the end of 1971. He finally succumbed to it in November 1974.

3

EYEBALL-TO-EYEBALL CONFRONTATION OVER CUBA

U Thant's greatest achievement in his ten-year tenure was his intervention in the Cuban missile crisis of October 1962, when the world came close to a nuclear holocaust. In this he was ably assisted by Omar Loutfi, a brilliant diplomat, who had joined his staff earlier that year.

It was after the Suez Crisis in 1956 that Loutfi, as Ambassador of Egypt (later to be called UAR, after the ill-fated merger with Syria) to the UN, established a close friendship with U Thant, then Ambassador of Burma to the UN.

When U Thant became Acting Secretary-General in November 1961, he looked around for a few trusted persons to appoint as principal advisers to assist him in his new and heavy task. He thought of Loutfi, but hesitated to approach him. There was a difference of $2,000 a month between his salary and allowances as Ambassador, and the maximum the UN could offer him as Under Secretary-General, the second highest post in the Secretariat. Also, as Ambassador he had a sumptuous apartment at the Plaza Hotel, paid for by his government. Loutfi was aware that U Thant was looking for a top man from the Arab Group, and we discussed the matter at length. Money was not an all-important issue, for he did not have a family to support and was well-off. Loutfi told me how highly he valued U Thant's counsel on international affairs; the rapport they had; that after seven hectic years as Representative of Egypt, working hard on many complex issues such as Suez, Palestine, Jordan-Lebanon and the Congo, he was tired and felt it was time for a change. His mind made up, Loutfi entrusted me to convey the message that he would be interested in the job. When I did this, U Thant said: 'I am delighted, Omar is the best of the lot.'

So in February 1962, Omar Loutfi made the change-over from an Ambassador representing his country to that of an international civil servant working for the world organisation as 'Under Secretary-General for Special Political Affairs.'

At their first meeting, Loutfi declared that to avoid any embarrassment to the Secretary-General, he should not handle any matter relating to Palestine. U Thant was happy to hear this and lost no time in passing the word to the Israeli Mission.

It was 10 a.m. on October 22, 1962, when Luis Foy, correspondent of the AFP and a friend came to my office in the press area of the UN building. Usually a casual person in attire and manner, with a ready smile, he was now unexpectedly solemn. He closed the door and said: 'I want you to convey to U Thant that Kennedy will address the nation with a very important statement on all TV networks at 7.00 p.m. today. It will deal with Cuba, but I have no details.'

I decided to wait for U Thant in the lobby of the UN Secretariat. As usual, there were correspondents waiting for him as he got out of his car, and I stayed until what was known as the 'lobby press conference' ended. At last we were in the elevator, together with his bodyguard. I said I had an important message. He ushered me to his office, closed the door and I gave him the news from notes. He listened carefully, and said that it was in line with other information he had received.

Adlai Stevenson, the United States Ambassador to the UN, came to see U Thant in the afternoon and confirmed that President Kennedy's statement would indeed concern Cuba.

That evening, it was a grave President who told the American people, and the world, that the Soviet Union was building bases in Cuba (which, in the excitement of the moment, he twice mispronounced as 'Cuber') capable of launching missiles carrying nuclear warheads which had a range of 2,000 miles. He also stated that the United States was asking for an emergency meeting of the UN Security Council to take up a resolution calling for the dismantling and withdrawal of all offensive weapons from Cuba.

Kennedy added that, with effect from the night of October 22, the United States would impose a naval and air quarantine on shipments of offensive military equipment to Cuba. Kennedy urged Khrushchev to withdraw the missiles and 'move the world back from the abyss of destruction'. It was eyeball-to-eyeball confrontation between the two superpowers.

The same evening, U Thant received from Ambassador Stevenson a request for an emergency meeting of the Security Council. This was followed by a request from Ambassador Zorin of the Soviet Union (President of the Council for the month), who accused the United States Government of 'violating the UN Charter and international law and increasing the threat of war'. Cuba, in turn, requested an emergency meeting of the Council to consider 'the act of war unilaterally committed by the US in ordering the blockade'.

The Security Council met on Tuesday, October 23. Several delegates from various groups had met urgently to discuss what could be done at that critical moment in world history.

Loutfi discussed with some of his former colleagues, Ambassadors from the non-aligned countries, what role the Secretary-General should play to ease the tension. What emerged was a consensus among representatives of forty-five delegations that U Thant should appeal directly to Chairman Khrushchev and President Kennedy. This was promptly reported to U Thant, who was keen on providing a formula to allow the Soviets and the Americans to withdraw from a dangerous confrontation without losing face. His inclination to do so was bolstered by the fact that he had held private talks as Secretary-General, in late August and early September, with both Khrushchev and Kennedy. He got on well, and had a good rapport, with both. When sceptics suggested that he was only Acting Secretary-General, and that if his appeal were rebuffed it would endanger the United Nations itself, he replied that such a suggestion was academic, for a nuclear war would end everything, including the UN.

The Security Council was deadlocked. Ambassador Stevenson stated that the transformation of Cuba into a base for offensive weapons was a threat to peace, and it was this which had led to the United States imposing a quarantine of Cuba. Ambassador Zorin retorted that the naval blockade and other military measures taken by the United States were a violation of the UN Charter and of international law. Cuba in turn rejected the United States charges, and said it had been forced to arm itself for defence against 'American aggression'.

The Council met on the night of October 24. Every seat was taken, and many delegates had to stand. The public gallery was filled to capacity. The atmosphere was tense. When U Thant spoke, there was complete silence in the audience and you could hear the shuffle of paper or someone clearing his throat. All cameras focused on his face.

THE APPEAL

U Thant said: 'Today the United Nations faces a moment of grave responsibility. What is at stake is not just the interests of the parties directly involved, nor just the interests of all member-states, but the very fate of mankind. If today the United Nations should prove itself ineffective, it may have proved itself so for all time. In the circumstances, not only as Acting Secretary-General of the United Nations but as a human being, I would be failing in my duty if I did not express my profound hope and conviction that moderation, self-restraint and good sense will prevail over all other considerations.

'In this situation where the very existence of mankind is in the balance, I derive some consolation from the fact that there is some common ground in the draft resolutions introduced in the Council. Irrespective of the fate of those draft resolutions, that common ground remains. It calls for urgent negotiations between the parties directly involved, though as I said earlier, the rest of the world is also an interested party. In this context, I cannot help expressing the view that some of the measures proposed or already taken, which the Council is called upon to approve, are very unusual and, I might say, even extraordinary except in wartime.

'I have sent the following identically worded messages to the President of the United States of America and the Chairman of the Council of Ministers of the USSR:

' "I have been asked by the permanent representatives of a large number of member-governments of the United Nations to address an urgent appeal to you in the present critical situation. These representatives feel that in the interest of international peace and security, all concerned should refrain from any action which may aggravate the situation and bring with it the risk of war.

' "In their view, it is important that time should be given to enable the parties concerned to get together with a view to resolving the present crisis peacefully and normalising the situation in the Caribbean. This involves, on the one hand, the voluntary suspension of all arms shipments to Cuba, and also the voluntary suspension of the quarantine measures involving the searching of ships bound for Cuba.

' "I believe that such voluntary suspension for a period of two to three weeks will greatly ease the situation and give time to the parties concerned to meet and discuss with a view to finding a peaceful solution of the problem. In this context, I shall make myself available to all parties for whatever services I may be able to perform. I urgently appeal to your Excellency to give immediate consideration to this message." '

U Thant continued: 'I should like also to take this occasion to address an urgent appeal to the president and prime minister of the Revolutionary Government of Cuba. Yesterday, Ambassador Garcia Inchaustegui of Cuba recalled the words of his president, words which were uttered from the rostrum of the General Assembly just over two weeks ago, and I quote: "If the United States could give assurances, by word and deed, that it would not commit acts of aggression against our country, we solemnly declare that there would be no need for our weapons and our armies . . ."

'Here again I feel that on the basis of discussion, some common ground may be found through which a way may be traced out of the present impasse. I believe it would also contribute greatly to the same end if the construction and development of major military facilities and installations in Cuba could be suspended during the period of negotiations.

'I now make a most solemn appeal to the parties concerned to enter into negotiations immediately, even this night if possible, irrespective of any other procedures which may be available or which could be invoked. I realise that if my appeal is heeded, the first subject to be discussed will be the modalities, and all parties concerned will have to agree to comply with those responsibilities which fall on them before any agreement as a whole can become effective. It would be shortsighted for the parties concerned to seek assurances on the end-result before the negotiations had even begun.

'During the seventeen years that have passed since the end of the Second World War, there has never been a more dangerous or closer confrontation of the major powers. At a time when the danger to world peace was less immediate, or so it appeared by comparison, my distinguished predecessor, Dag Hammarskjöld, said: "The principles of the Charter are, by far, greater than the Organisation in which they are embodied, and the aims which they are to safeguard are holier than the policies of any single nation, or people." He went on to say: "Discretion and impartiality imposed on the Secretary-General by the character of his immediate task may not degenerate into a policy of expediency . . . A Secretary-General cannot serve on any other assumption than that – within the necessary limits of human frailty and honest differences of opinion – all member-nations honour their pledge to observe all articles of the Charter." '

U Thant concluded: 'It is after considerable deliberations that I have decided to send the two messages to which I referred earlier, and likewise I have decided to make this brief intervention tonight before the Security Council, including the appeal to the President and Prime Minister of Cuba. I hope that at this moment, not only in the Council Chamber but in the world outside, good sense and understanding will be placed above the anger of the moment or the pride of nations. The path of negotiation and compromise is the only course by which the peace of the world can be secured at this critical moment.'*

When he had finished, he looked towards the President of the Council (Zorin of the Soviet Union) and said, 'Thank you, Mr President.' Immediately, and by prior agreement with U Thant, Ambassador Frederick Boland, the representative of Ireland in the Security Council, moved the adjournment of the meeting. Zorin looked angry, and his anger grew as he saw delegates lining up to congratulate U Thant. A little later, Zorin managed to take U Thant aside, seeking to talk to him. But it was already late at night, and U Thant was exhausted. He asked Zorin to come the next morning, and left the Security Council Chamber with Loutfi to return to his office on the thirty-eighth floor.

The following morning at 10 a.m., Zorin came with his Deputy Ambassador Morozov and an interpreter. He lodged a strong protest against the appeal, because 'U Thant did not condemn the United States blockade'. Bluntly, U Thant asked whether the Ambassador was protesting on instructions from his government, or was he speaking in his personal capacity. Zorin was taken aback and did not answer. Pressing his point, U Thant hinted that he might as well send a message to Moscow explaining how hard he was trying to be impartial and request a clarification of the protest. U Thant in fact sent a message to Moscow through Victor Lessiovsky, a Soviet official in the UN Secretariat who was rumoured to be the KGB agent. Whether Lessiovsky delivered it or not we were not sure, but apparently he did. For it was about forty-eight hours later that Khrushchev informed U Thant that he was sending Vassily Kuznetsov, First Deputy Foreign Minister, to head the Soviet Delegation in the negotiations with the United States.

That same afternoon, Ambassador Morozov asked to see U Thant urgently, and gave him a copy of a cable from Chairman Khrushchev. It was friendly and positive. He wrote: 'Dear U Thant . . . I have received your message and have carefully studied the proposal it contains. I welcome your initiative . . . I agree to your proposal!' U Thant immediately understood why Morozov had come alone. Zorin had made his protest without instructions, and after Khrushchev's message he would know that U Thant was now aware of his *faux pas*. When U Thant discussed this episode with Loutfi, the latter ventured the opinion that Zorin was perhaps an innocent victim in as much as he was completely in the dark – that he had not known about the presence of the

*Security Council official records, 17th year – 1024th meeting.

missiles in Cuba and had protested in the belief that Moscow would reject U Thant's appeal.

Before the Zorin meeting, on October 25, U Thant had followed up his appeal in the Security Council by sending further cables to the two leaders. He asked Khrushchev to instruct Soviet ships, already on their way to Cuba, to stay away from the interception area for a limited time to permit discussions of the modalities of a possible agreement to settle the problem peacefully in line with the UN Charter.

The following day, October 26, U Thant received a reply from Khrushchev, which again started with 'Dear U Thant'. It expressed appreciation of U Thant's efforts to avert military action, accepted his proposal, and stated that masters of Soviet vessels bound for Cuba had been ordered to stay out of the interception area. It concluded: 'Your efforts to ensure world peace will always meet with understanding and support on our part.'

To President Kennedy, U Thant's cable stated that Soviet ships would be ordered to stay out of the interception area, and urged that instructions be issued to United States vessels in the Caribbean 'to do everything possible to avoid direct confrontation with Soviet ships in order to minimise the risk of any untoward incident'.

In replying, Kennedy welcomed U Thant's efforts and declared that since the Soviet government had accepted his proposal, the US government would abide by the request that American vessels do everything possible to avoid direct confrontation.

On October 26, U Thant sent a cable to Castro informing him that encouraging responses to his appeal for negotiations had been received, and urged that the construction and development of major military facilities and installations in Cuba, especially those designed to launch medium-and intermediate-range ballistic missiles, be suspended during the period of negotiations that were under way.

On October 27, U Thant received a reply from Castro stating that Cuba was prepared to discuss its differences with the United States. After denouncing the blockade as an 'act of war', he declared that Cuba would be prepared to accept the compromises suggested as efforts for peace, provided that the United States desisted from threats and aggressive actions against Cuba, including the blockade. Castro invited U Thant to visit Cuba for direct discussions on the crisis.

Replying to Castro, U Thant expressed his gratitude for the positive reply and accepted the invitation to go to Havana 'to continue our common effort toward the peaceful solution of the problem'.

On October 28, U Thant sent a cable, informing Khrushchev that he had accepted Castro's invitation to visit Havana, and added: 'I am gratified to note that you have already instructed your officers to stop the building of missile bases, to dismantle them and to return the missiles to the Soviet Union.'

On the US side, Ambassador Stevenson handed U Thant a *note verbale* that the United States accepted the Soviet proposals to remove the missiles under possible United Nations observation. In return, the United States would agree to lift the blockade and to pledge not to invade Cuba.

Moreover, Castro, who was not a party to the US-Soviet understanding, was bitter. On October 28, he sent a cable to U Thant saying that the guarantees offered by Kennedy were insufficient unless the United States fulfilled five measures – 'cessation of the economic blockade; cessation of all subversive activities; cessation of piratical attacks from Puerto Rico; cessation of the violation of Cuban airspace; and withdrawal of US forces from Guantanamo*'.

This cable, which threatened in effect to sabotage the flimsy understanding reached between the Soviets and the Americans, made U Thant's visit to Havana more urgent. Meanwhile President Kennedy had designated John McCloy, a close associate, to head the American team and assist Stevenson at about the same time that Vassily Kuznetsov arrived in New York as head of the Soviet Delegation. Press reports of a possible United States pre-emptive strike against Cuba continued unabated, which made the Cubans more nervous than ever.

Against this background, U Thant left New York for Havana on the morning of October 30 on a Varig (Brazilian Airlines) plane chartered by the United Nations. He had with him an unusually large party. Group one, travelling with him, consisted of seventeen people including security officers and radio operators – he had hoped to persuade Castro to allow UN observers to remain behind to supervise the withdrawal of the missiles from Cuba.

On the same plane, the eager UN people had packed twenty-eight large cases containing communications equipment, supplies, typewriters and other paraphernalia needed to set up a 'UN mission'. In the excitement of the hurried arrangements, the person in charge in 'General Services' neglected to clear this with U Thant. Heading the list of those

---

*The large US naval base in south-eastern Cuba, established by treaty in 1903, which the United States has continued to occupy since the 1959 Revolution.

who accompanied him on the flight were: Omar Loutfi, Hernane Tavares de Sa (Brazilian head of the Office of Public Information), Brigadier Indar J. Rikhye (Military Adviser), Miguel Marin as interpreter, and myself as press officer for the Secretary-General. Also in the party were Donald Thomas, personal aide and chief of security, and a secretary.

Group two comprised nineteen people: military staff, radio engineers, telex operators, interpreters and an information officer. They had assembled in New York and were ready to leave, on a second chartered plane, once they had received the green light from the Secretary-General after his talks in Cuba.

On arrival at Havana airport in the early afternoon, U Thant was met by a large delegation headed by Foreign Minister Raul Roa. There was maximum security, and although several armed guards surrounded the plane, the reception was friendly. When the formalities were over, and just before we got into a convoy of American limousines waiting to take us to the guest houses, an army major in battle fatigues whispered into the Foreign Minister's ear. A few remarks were exchanged between the two men, and the major saluted and left.

Raul Roa accompanied U Thant in the first car. During the journey, the Foreign Minister asked about the large boxes, carrying the UN emblem, which had been unloaded from the plane. U Thant, extremely embarrassed, said that he did not know about them but would certainly find out. By the time we reached the villa, soldiers were busy storing them neatly under a shed in a corner of the garden.

U Thant went to his suite and summoned Donald Thomas to enquire about the boxes. Thomas did not know either, and suggested that Rikhye might know: Rikhye assumed that the cases contained communication and office equipment. Although U Thant did not show any anger, for he was always able to control his feelings, he was furious. The UN Secretariat had been gravely mistaken to behave so presumptiously at such a tense moment by bringing all that equipment without the authorisation of the Secretary-General and the explicit agreement of the Cubans.

In discussing the problem, Loutfi surmised that since the boxes had been brought to the villa by soldiers, they must have been carefully examined *en route*, and the Cubans would know what they contained. He advised that the truth should be told: that they had been loaded without U Thant's permission, and would be returned to the plane. Nothing should be allowed to mar the crucial talks with Castro which were to take place in an hour's time.

The talks started at 3 p.m. at the presidential palace. On the Cuban side were President Osvaldo Dorticos, Premier Fidel Castro, Foreign Minister Raul Roa and Ambassador Mario Garcia Inchaustegui. On U Thant's side were Omar Loutfi, Hernan Tavares de Sa, Brigadier Rikhye and Miguel Marin, the interpreter.

After underlining the gravity of the situation, U Thant made a strong plea for a United Nations supervision of the dismantling of the missile bases and their removal as agreed by Khrushchev. He stressed the importance of the United States pledges to lift the blockade and not take military action against Cuba. Castro was adamant. He reiterated his accusations against the 'aggression' of the United States, and declared that Cuba would not accept any UN supervision.

The talks lasted for two hours and there was no hint of agreement. Quietly Loutfi, sitting on U Thant's right, passed a note saying 'we are not getting anywhere – do you wish to propose to meet Castro alone tomorrow?' U Thant decided to follow this advice and made the proposal. Castro immediately agreed.

Back at the villa, U Thant was told that the Soviet Ambassador in Havana wanted to see him. In fact he was waiting in one of the reception rooms. The Ambassador thanked U Thant for his efforts for a peaceful settlement of the crisis, and added that instructions had been received from Moscow to dismantle the missiles and their launching-pads. The Ambassador asked if he could bring the Soviet general in charge of the missiles, who was waiting outside, to attend the meeting. A tall, blond man entered the room. U Thant asked the General when the missiles would be dismantled. Without hesitation, the General replied that the dismantling of the missiles and their bases had started and would be completed three days later (on Friday, November 2). U Thant was elated with the news. It was obvious that the Ambassador and the General were acting on specific orders from Moscow.

After the meeting, U Thant asked Loutfi, Rikhye and me to join him to brief us on what had transpired. Loutfi's immediate reaction was that judging from the tone of the earlier meeting with the Cubans, Castro had not known that the Soviet Ambassador was coming to see U Thant. He would find out in due course, since the villa was under surveillance and the secret police would recognise the Ambassador. Loutfi was inclined to think that this encounter should be kept confidential until we had left Havana, and U Thant would then announce to the world that the Soviet missiles were being removed from Cuba.

Under the circumstances, as the person in charge of press relations, I suggested that I telephone New York with a press release, outlining briefly the formal meeting between the Cuban leaders and the UN delegation, and adding that the 'discussions were fruitful and conducted in a friendly atmosphere', and nothing else. U Thant agreed and instructed me to do this.

The following morning, October 31, U Thant went to the presidential palace at 10 a.m., accompanied only by his interpreter. Castro was bitter against Khrushchev's decision to dismantle the missiles without consulting Havana. He informed U Thant that he was going on the air to give his account of the crisis. U Thant argued against any move that might worsen the situation, and urged him to delay the speech. Castro refused to postpone the speech, but promised to delete certain parts attacking Khrushchev for accepting the proposal of United Nations inspection of the missile sites in Cuba.

U Thant then asked if Castro would agree to our leaving behind in Havana one or two UN aides to provide direct liaison between the Cuban Government and the Secretary-General during the crisis. Castro refused; he did not want UN inspection or presence because that would be a violation of Cuba's sovereignty.

Towards the end of the meeting, U Thant asked Castro, on humanitarian grounds, to return a Major Rudolph Anderson, a US Airforce pilot whose U2 had been shot down by the Cubans with a Soviet missile on October 27. Castro replied that Anderson had been killed when his plane violated Cuba's airspace, but agreed to return the body. Throughout the meeting not a word was mentioned about U Thant's conversation with the Soviet Ambassador. (A comprehensive summary record of this meeting, corrected by U Thant himself, immediately follows this chapter. It has never previously been published.)

U Thant went back to the villa for lunch. Before sitting down at the table he instructed Rikhye to call Narasimhan, in New York. Because the telephones were tapped, Rikhye spoke to his compatriot in Hindi and Urdu. He requested that the second UN group should not come to Cuba.

The Varig 707 took off for New York on the afternoon of October 31 with U Thant and his party. Reviewing the results of his talks, U Thant concluded that although he had failed to persuade Castro to accept UN inspection, as demanded by the United States and accepted by the Soviet Union, the visit should be considered a success since he had acquired first-hand information about the dismantling of the missiles and their eventual return to the Soviet Union. This alone, once announced to the world, would help to calm the war hysteria that was sweeping the United States and creating an atmosphere of tension throughout the world. As for inspection, it was a matter to be negotiated with McCloy and Kuznetsov in New York.

U Thant had just completed correcting a draft for a press statement I had prepared, when Loutfi said something to him. It was a reminder to include a reference to the fact that Castro had agreed to return the body of the American pilot, Major Anderson, to the United States.

We arrived at Idlewild Airport, New York, on the night of October 31. A police escort rushed us to the airport press room, which was packed with reporters, photographers and TV cameras. U Thant read his statement slowly and carefully. He said: 'I return from Havana after fruitful discussions with the leaders of Cuba. These discussions were conducted strictly in the context of my correspondence with Premier Fidel Castro, resulting from the proceedings of the Security Council meetings. There was agreement that the United Nations should continue to participate in the peaceful settlement of the problem.'

He continued: 'During my stay in Havana, I was reliably informed that the dismantling of the missiles and their installations was already in progress and that this process should be completed by Friday, November 2. Thereafter, there would come their shipment and return to the Soviet Union, arrangements for which are understood to be in hand. One last word. At my request, the Cuban government has agreed to return, on humanitarian grounds, the body of Major Anderson to the United States.'

He finished reading. There were no questions. The reporters scrambled to the telephones to dictate their stories which were published under banner headlines the next morning. Back at his office, U Thant received a summary in English of Castro's speech to the Cuban people. He had kept his word. It was a mild speech which referred to disagreements and different approaches between two allies (the Soviet Union and Cuba).

To help soothe Castro, Moscow dispatched Anastas Mikoyan, Soviet Deputy Prime Minister, to Havana. En route, he made a one-day stopover in New York, held a meeting with U Thant on November 1, and gave a press conference to deny to the world that there was any rift between the Soviet Union and Cuba. Mikoyan was a clever performer. He knew how to field embarrassing questions from reporters, and succeeded in giving the impression that the crisis was over.

Meanwhile, the negotiations between McCloy and Kuznetsov, with their respective delegations, were proceeding smoothly in U Thant's conference room on the thirty-eighth floor of the UN building. The United States dropped its insistence on UN inspection of the dismantling of the missile launching-pads in Cuba in exchange for US observation flights without Cuban interference.

On November 20, 1962, President Kennedy announced that Chairman Khrushchev had informed him that the IL28 Soviet bombers were being removed from Cuba and had agreed that this could be monitored by United States reconnaissance flights. The same day Kennedy ordered the blockade lifted.

On January 7, 1963, U Thant received an unprecedented joint letter signed by Stevenson and Kuznetsov.[*] It read: 'On behalf of the Governments of the United States of America and the Soviet Union, we desire to express to you our appreciation for your efforts in assisting our Governments to avert the serious threat to peace which recently arose in the Caribbean area. While it has not been possible for our Governments to resolve all the problems that have arisen in connection with this affair, they believe that in view of the degree of understanding reached between them on the settlement of the crisis and the extent of progress in the implementation of this understanding, it is not necessary for this item to occupy further the attention of the Security Council at this time.

'The Governments of the United States of America and of the Soviet Union express the hope that the actions taken to avert the threat of war in connection with the crisis will lead toward the adjustment of other differences between them and the general easing of tensions that could cause a further threat of war.'

U Thant hastened to reply on January 9, thanking the two governments and sharing their hope that the action taken to avert the threat of war would lead to the adjustment of other differences between them. On his instructions, both letters were issued as Security Council documents, thus heralding the end of the crisis.

In the years that followed, U Thant, while capitalising on his role and the usefulness of the United Nations in that dangerous situation, never failed to pay warm tribute to the sense of responsibility and statesmanship displayed by Kennedy and Khrushchev in those tense weeks in October–November 1962. That, he maintained, had been the main factor in the success of his intervention.

---

[*]UN Security Council document S 7/01/1963.

The heading of the following document is self-explanatory. The handwritten corrections are U Thant's own.

CONFIDENTIAL.

Notes on my Second meeting with Premier Fidel Castro of Cuba in Havana on the 31st of October, 1962.

Present:

President Dorticós, Premier Fidel Castro and Foreign Minister Roa. On my side I attended the meeting alone, without any aides.

Castro was in a bitter mood. He was angry both with Premier Khrushchev and President Kennedy. He started the meeting with a long statement denouncing Premier Khrushchev for having given a pledge to President Kennedy to demolish the missile sights in Cuba and their withdrawal from Cuban soil without getting prior agreement from the Government of Cuba. He stressed the fact that Cuba is an independent sovereign state and anything involving Cuban territory belonged legitimately to the Cuban Government. Since Khrushchev had already made a commitment to Kennedy to demolish and withdraw the missiles already installed on Cuban soil without the knowledge and consent of the Cuban Government, there was no alternative for him than to denounce the Soviet Government publicly.

The United States Government also breached the United Nations Charter by its quarantine, thus shutting off Cuba from the

outside world. I asked him about the inspection of the
missile ~~sights~~ by the United Nations which was the primary
purpose of my visit to Havana, He said that his government
would strongly oppose any inspection of Cuban territory by
a third party although he was a believer in the United
Nations. He reiterated his arguments given on the previous day.

He also added that the United Nations ~~can~~ inspect anything
outside the Cuban territorial waters. He asked me to
convey his views both to the Soviet Union and the United
States. He then disclosed to me that only the previous
night he had informed the Cuban people on Havana radio
that he would make a public policy statement from the radio
on that night (31st October 1962).

I told Castro that since he was a believer in the United
Nations it was a test case for the efficacy of the United
Nations if his government refused to permit the inspection
of missile ~~sights~~ by the United Nations, ~~then~~ I foresaw
disastrous consequences and even war seemed to be inevitable.
Hence Castro knew, my military advisor Major General Indar
Jit Rikhye was also with me and ~~who~~ attended the first
meeting ~~that~~ previous day, and that his presence in Havana
was just to discuss with the Cuban military authorities
regarding the modalities of United Nations inspection. If
he refused to permit United Nations inspection of missile
~~sights~~, I made it clear to him that I had no alternative

[handwritten margin annotations: "sites", "a matter of routine", "Give up on the first day of meeting.", "and that", "As", "the", "sites,"]

but to report to the Security Council about the failure of my mission and why it failed. Such a permission would calm the atmosphere which was very tense and even explosive, and I appealed to him to reconsider his position. I also requested him to postpone his proposed radio statement that night since that would create more difficulties all around.

Castro said that he had already announced on the radio the previous night that he would make a public announcement on the radio on the 31st of October. The most he could do was to postpone the announcement by one day; that means the announcement would be made on the 1st of November. He explained to me that the Cuban people were waiting eagerly for his announcement and would never understand if no such announcement was made.

I replied to him that as soon as I got back to New York I would convey his government's decision to the Government of the United States immediately and that it would be advisable to wait for the reaction of the United States before he announced his policy statement on the radio.

Castro said it was too late now. He agreed to postpone the announcement by one day because of my presence in Havana and because of my request. In his view if no such announce- ments were made, the people would be puzzled and that the and continue Cuban public might even think his government had changed its policy.

I told him that I agreed that Khrushchev should have ~~dis~~ consulted ~~cussed with~~ him about the demolition and withdrawal of Soviet missiles from Cuban territory before he made his pledge to President Kennedy, but it was too late now for me to tell the Soviet Government ~~about its failure to get~~ ~~prior agreement from the Cuban Government.~~ I also told him that the inspection of the missiles by the United Nations outside the Cuban territorial waters was not a practical proposition. There would be many problems; particularly the United States would still suspect that some missile ~~sights~~ would still be left behind on Cuban territory even if the United Nations could verify the number and type of missiles removed from Cuba. Regarding the radio broadcast, my suggestion was that the Prime Minister could go on air that night and explain to his people that the proposed public statement would be postponed indefinitely at the request of the Secretary General who was trying to seek a peaceful solution to that very delicate problem. I appealed to him to exercise restraint and not to create more difficulties in finding a just and peaceful solution to the problem. I assured him that if he did not broadcast his

-2-

speech that night it might have a calming effect on all parties. I also told him that in short terms the results would not be obvious but in the long run restraint would create conditions for a peaceful solution. I told him that my appeal to him to exercise the utmost restraint in his pronouncement would be one aspect of my recommendations to the Security Council. I also told him that the Security Council would be faced with a very serious situation if all sides were to take military decisions.

Castro replied that the 5 point proposal he made would be the only basis on which a just and lasting peace could be established. As far as his government was concerned there was no alternative but to discuss only within the framework of the 5 point proposal. He knew that the Security Council would be faced with a very difficult situation which the delegate to the United Nations would press for the 5 points in the Security Council. He reiterated his government's position that Cuba would never accept any solution but a status quo; that was the quarantine of the island and the demolition and withdrawal of the missiles from Cuba without the knowledge and consent of his government. Whether to keep or not to keep the missiles on Cuban soil was within the sole prerogative of the Cuban Government. He said that Cuba had no agressive intentions while the United States definitely had such intentions. He pledged his government's allegiance to the United Nations Charter and international law and equal rights of all states large and small.

I asked him if he could suggest any date for a Security Council meeting at which perhaps his Foreign Minister could be present.

Castro said any date would suit him. Perhaps, he said, Wednesday the 7th of November would be a good date.

I told him not to be over-exercised by the United States' intentions. I reminded him that it was the election year and time for Presidential campaigns and usually the United States had to take a tough line on such issues since the people in the United States were getting very emotional on such issues. I also told him that before I left New York this view was shared by many delegates at the United Nations.

Then I asked him whether I could leave behind one or two men from my team to serve as a link between me and his government. I tried to convince him that such presence would be highly desirable since the international community would feel that the Government of Cuba had agreed to permit the United Nations representatives on its soil for the purpose of contact and communication.

3

Castro said he was sorry he could not permit anybody to stay behind in Cuba. He explained that such a presence would be interpreted by the people of Cuba as dealing with inspection, and the issue of inspection was rejected by everybody in his country. He said Cuba would send a mission to the United Nations and that his Foreign Minister would be in the United Nations for high level negotiations with the appropriate governments. In his view contacts between me and his government would be better served in New York than in Havana.

I told him that as the head of a sovereign government I had to respect his views and promised to take back with me all those who accompanied me to Havana.

I then asked him about the United States Air Force pilot was was reported to be captured by the Cuban authorities when his plane was shot down.

Castro said the Cuban missiles had shot down a United States plane and it fell on Cuban grounds and that the United States pilot was dead when he was found. If he were alive he would be agreeable to send him back to the U.S. He said Cuba could never accept the legalization of air intrusion over Cuban territory by any power. He asked me to tell the

United States Government to stop over-flights since they were
provocations. According to him there were daily over-flights
and he told me that his armed forces would shoot down any
plane which trespassed his country's air space. His people
were very indignant over such provative acts. I told him
many delegates at the United Nations were in agreement
that over-flights by any power over another country were
not legal, but at the same time I told him that it would
be necessary to understand the feelings in the United
States regarding the installation of Soviet missiles over
Cuban territory/meant primarily for/targets in the United
States.

(margin note: specific)

(left margin note: which were considered to him)

Castro then said the blockade of Cuba in the high seas and
over-flights by the United States Air Force were both
illegal and intolerable. He said the delegations should
also take these factors into account. He said the root
cause of the conflict and crisis was the quarantine and over-
flights.

I assured him that I would convey this information to the
United States as soon as I got back to New York,

-4-

Castro said he visited Havana Provence twice and on both
occasions he saw American planes flying over his head,
and it was very difficult for his military people to
refrain from firing at them, because according to him,
the Cuban people were "passionately patriotic".

I then reverted to the subject of the dead American pilot.
I asked him if purely on humanitarian grounds and for the
sake of the pilot's family, if the dead body could be sent
back to the United States. As a gesture of good-will I
requested him to comply with my request.

He said that because of my appeal he would issue instructions
immediately to send back the dead body to the United States.
He said that the American pilot had a parachute, but obviously had no time to use it since the plane got a direct hit.

Then I brought up another subject regarding the United
Nations technical assistance to Cuba as in the case of other
member states. I asked him if he were satisfied with the
operation of the technicians from the United Nations in
their respective fields. He said he was satisfied with
their performance.

Before I left him I wanted to make one point very clear: whether
that his government would not discuss any other plan
besides the 5 points presented by him. Castro told me it

& he said.

was true. The 5 point proposal was based on logic and
reality tion, He added that the United States Government
had been saying that Guatanamo Base was in Cuba with the
agreement of the Cuban Government. However, he said that
the government who had agreed to this was no longer there;
it was only logical that the new government must review the
agreement. He also said that the conference of non-aligned
governments in Belgrade last September, also agreed with
his point of view. He said that the Belgrade conference
decided against all foreign military bases on foreign
countries.

& I said.

I asked him if he had any further observations besides
the issues keath. He said his government would do everything
according to the Charter of the United Nations and that
his government respected the Secretary General's positive
action for the achievement of peace according to the Charter.
He expressed his thanks for my visit to Havana to ease
tensions and he asked me to take back to the United Nations
the position of the Cuban people that it would try its best
to maintain national serenity sovereignty.

He then asked me if the records of the meetings of the previous
day and today should be released. I suggested to him that
for obvious reasons the records of the previous day's meetings
should be released but today's meeting should be regarded as

-5-

purely private and confidential. He agreed.

He concluded his remarks by saying that small countries were in danger of being overpowered by major powers and so small countries should be very jealous of their independence and sovereignty. He said his people were prepared for any sacrifice. His country was small but his people believed in honor and prestige. He would not only defend the honor and prestige of his country but the honor and prestige and rights of all small countries in the world. He said once *~~we felt~~* all small countries would fall.

Castro said that even now the United States' invasion of Cuba could not be ruled out; there were many aggressive elements in the United States whose main purpose was to topple him and install a government friendly towards Washington. He added that the Pentagon is now more powerful than before because of this crisis.

4

VIETNAM: THE QUEST FOR PEACE

Until the spring of 1964, U Thant had carefully avoided expressing substantive opinion on the situation in Southeast Asia except for his statement, at a news conference on September 12, 1963, on the absence of democratic processes in South Vietnam. His first major comment on the nature of the Vietnam conflict was made at a press conference in Paris on April 29, 1964. In the light of future developments, the views he expressed then showed a profound understanding of the situation. But his words were not heeded. U Thant expressed the conviction that military methods would not solve the problem. 'As I see the problem in Southeast Asia . . . it is not essentially military, it is political, and therefore political and diplomatic means alone, in my view, can solve it.'

He elaborated on these views at another press conference in Ottawa on May 26, 1964. Citing the Geneva Agreement of 1954 as an example of the sort of political solution he had in mind, he said that he was not sure whether the terms accepted in 1954 could again be put to the test ten years later. 'The right solution at the right time could yield the right results,' he maintained. 'But the right solution at the wrong time could well prove to be futile.'

As he was in later years, U Thant was sceptical about the feasibility of a United Nations role in Southeast Asia, both because of the limitations of its authority and resources, and because neither South nor North Vietnam was a member of the UN; and the People's Republic of China, which exercised a considerable influence on Hanoi, had not yet acceded to the seat of China at the UN.

Yet the war in Vietnam – 'the cruel, bloody senseless conflict' as he often referred to it –'haunted him throughout his ten years as Secretary-General. As an Asian and a Buddhist, he was obsessed with finding a peaceful solution. Vietnam featured in all his talks with world leaders during his official visits, and sometimes dominated them. He discussed the conflict at different times with Khrushchev, General de Gaulle and President Johnson.

In August 1964, during a visit to Washington, U Thant sounded out Secretary of State Dean Rusk on the possibility of a meeting, face to face, between representatives from Washington and Hanoi. Feeling that

Rusk was receptive, he took the initiative in contacting Hanoi and sent a message to President Ho Chi Minh, through Moscow, that it would be in the interests of peace if a representative of Hanoi would meet a representative from Washington without any publicity whatsoever.

Four weeks later, a positive reply came from Hanoi. A jubilant U Thant immediately informed Ambassador Adlai Stevenson, who passed the information to Washington. While waiting for a decision, Stevenson asked U Thant to suggest a venue for the meeting. U Thant proposed Rangoon and discussed the matter with the representative of Burma to the UN, who cabled his government asking if it would be acceptable. The Burmese government agreed, and U Thant phoned Stevenson with the 'good news'. A few days later, on January 30, 1965, a sad Stevenson came to see U Thant to say that Washington had had second thoughts and would not agree. They felt that such a meeting could not be kept secret, and if the news leaked out, the government of South Vietnam in Saigon would collapse.

In the months that followed, U Thant found out that his initiative had been turned down by Dean Rusk, the Secretary of State, and had never been referred to President Johnson. This failure put an end to the use of the good offices of the Secretary-General in finding a peaceful solution of the Vietnam war.

But U Thant was not totally discouraged. In March 1965, in response to a question at the noon press briefing, he authorised me to say that the Secretary-General was putting forward a three-point peace proposal: (1) cessation of the bombing of North Vietnam; (2) de-escalation of all military activities by all parties in South Vietnam; and (3) participation of all those who were fighting in South Vietnam in any discussions for a peaceful settlement.

Hanoi's initial response was guarded. It stressed that the bombing had to cease without any pre-conditions, and ignored the other points. Peking reacted with a blast against the United Nations, calling it a 'tool of the United States'.

Meanwhile, U Thant took it upon himself to have a secret meeting with representatives of North Vietnam to seek their views first-hand. He had the first such meeting in Paris in April 1966, and the second in Rangoon in 1967. The latter was arranged in advance, and Hanoi sent a high-level delegation to talk with U Thant on March 2, 1967. The North Vietnamese delegation was headed by Colonel Ha Van Lau, deputy chief of the Hanoi Foreign Ministry. U Thant presented new proposals, which were an elaboration of his original three-point plan.

Back in New York, he waited for ten days and decided to formulate his new proposals. He circulated them, as an aide-memoire, on March 14: they were sent to the United States, North Vietnam, South Vietnam and the National Liberation Front. In spite of the secrecy pledged by all parties, news leaked out that U Thant had made new proposals, and I was bombarded with questions at the regular press briefing. All I could say was that I would pass the queries on to the Secretary-General and come back with an answer. Rumours and speculation were rife, and finally U Thant decided to devote a press conference, already scheduled for March 28, 1967, to Vietnam. He started by reading a prepared statement, as follows:

'Since we last met there has been more death, destruction, devastation and consequent misery, increasing at a more rapid rate than in any comparable period in the past, and there is an even greater danger of the war spreading beyond the frontiers of Vietnam. While the United Nations at present seems incapable of dealing with the war, many governments and personalities have been trying to bring about conditions for the transfer of the conflict from the battlefield to the conference table, so far without success. As Secretary-General of the United Nations I am distressed lest the prolongation of this war bring about a suffocation of this Organisation and in the end seriously affect the détente and co-operation among all nations.

'Since my return to New York in the first week of March, a good deal of speculation has focused on my reported new proposals to end the Vietnam war. Some capitals have even come out with public reactions to those proposals. When this press conference was arranged for today, it was far from my intention to make those proposals public, but, in view of the widespread interest shown in those proposals, and in view of certain reactions which are likely to confuse the general public regarding my sincere desire for peace, I have now decided to make those proposals public.

'It is for the world community to judge and assess those proposals against the background of the growing fury of the war, with definite prospects of involving larger areas of Asia. I have already received in writing the reactions of the parties principally involved, which I must continue to regard as confidential, and therefore I cannot comment upon them.

'My purpose in presenting those proposals was only to try to find, if possible, a common ground among the participants in the conflict, in view of the known reactions to my earlier three-point proposals. However, I would emphasise that I continue to regard my three-point proposals as representing the most useful first steps in preventing further escalation and intensification of the war and in beginning the reverse process of de-escalation and negotiations. In particular I have never ceased to consider that the bombing of North Vietnam constitutes an insurmountable obstacle to discussions. I also stand by my conviction that Vietnam is a political problem, which no amount of force will solve – and, after all, previous military measures have not succeeded in bringing about any talks.

'Therefore, while it is all too clear that the positions of the parties have never been so far apart, I have continued, and intend to continue, my efforts. I wish particularly, at this stage, to urge all responsible world leaders not to resign themselves to permitting a further aggravation of the situation.

'The obstacles to peace may be enormous, but it is not true, even at this stage, that negotiations would necessarily fail. A settlement respecting the principles agreed upon at Geneva and the realities of Vietnam, and yet safeguarding the long-term interests of all concerned, is not beyond reach. Such a settlement would at last open the way for the new, far-reaching initiatives in other fields urgently needed today.

'Now I shall read to you the proposals which, on March 14, in the form of an aide-memoire, I presented to the parties directly involved in the Vietnam conflict. Its text reads as follows:

'On many occasions in the past, the Secretary-General of the United Nations has expressed his very great concern about the conflict in Vietnam. That concern is intensified by the growing fury of the war, resulting in the increasing loss of lives, indescribable suffering and misery of the people, appalling devastation of the country, uprooting of society, astronomical sums spent on the war, and last but not least, his deepening anxiety over the increasing threat to the peace of the world. For these reasons, in the past three years or so, he submitted ideas and proposals to the parties primarily involved in the war, with a view to creating conditions congenial to negotiations, which unhappily have not been accepted by the parties. The prospects for peace seem to be more distant today than ever before.

'Nevertheless, the Secretary-General reasserts his conviction that a cessation of the bombing of North Vietnam continues to be a vital need, for moral and humanitarian reasons, and also because it is the step which could lead the way to meaningful talks to end the war.

'The situation being as it is today, the Secretary-General has now in mind proposals envisaging three steps:

'(a) a general stand-still truce;

'(b) preliminary talks;

'(c) reconvening of the Geneva Conference.

'In the view of the Secretary-General, a halt to all military activities by all sides is a practical necessity if useful negotiations are to be undertaken. Since the Secretary-General's three-point plan has not been accepted by the parties, he believes that a general stand-still truce by all parties to the conflict is now the only course which could lead to fruitful negotiations. It must be conceded that a truce without effective supervision is apt to be breached from time to time by one side or another, but an effective supervision of a truce, at least for the moment, seems difficult to envisage as a practical possibility.

'If the parties directly involved in the conflict are genuinely motivated by considerations of peace and justice, it is only to be expected that earnest efforts will be exerted to enforce the truce to the best of their ability. Should a public appeal by the Secretary-General in his personal capacity facilitate the observance of such a truce, he would gladly be prepared to do so. Appeals to that effect by a group of countries would also be worthy of consideration.

'Once the appeal has been made and a general stand-still truce comes into effect, the parties directly involved in the conflict should take the next step of entering into preliminary talks. While these talks are in progress, it is clearly desirable that the general stand-still truce should continue to be observed.

'In the view of the Secretary-General, these talks can take any of the following forms:

'(1) direct talks between the United States of America and the Democratic Republic of Vietnam;

'(2) direct talks between the two governments mentioned in (1) above, with the participation of the two Co-Chairmen of the Geneva Conference of 1954;

'(3) direct talks between the two governments mentioned in (1) above, with the participation of the members of the International Control Commission;

'(4) direct talks between the two governments mentioned in (1) above, with the participation of the two Co-Chairmen of the Geneva Conference of 1954 and of the members of the International Control Commission.

'The Secretary-General believes that these preliminary talks should aim at reaching an agreement on the modalities for the reconvening of the Geneva Conference, with the sole purpose of returning to the essentials of that agreement as repeatedly expressed by all parties to the conflict. These preliminary talks should seek to reach an agreement on the timing, place, agenda and participants in the subsequent formal meeting – the reconvening of the Geneva Conference.

'The Secretary-General deems it necessary to stress that the question of participants in the formal negotiations should not obstruct the way to a settlement. It is a question which could be solved only by agreeing that no fruitful discussions on ending the war in Vietnam could take place without involving all those who are actually fighting.

'Since the government of Saigon, as well as the National Front of Liberation of South Vietnam, are actually engaged in military operations, it is the view of the Secretary-General that a future formal conference could not usefully discuss the effective termination of all military activities and the new political situation that would result in South Vietnam, without the participation of representatives of the government in Saigon and representatives of the National Liberation Front of South Vietnam.

'In transmitting these proposals to the parties directly concerned, the Secretary-General believes that he is acting within the limits of his good offices purely in his private capacity. He hopes that the divergent positions held by the parties both on the nature of the conflict and the ultimate political objectives will not prevent them from giving their very serious attention to these proposals. Indeed, he takes this opportunity to appeal to them to give their urgent consideration to his proposals.'*

But these proposals were not acceptable. In April 1967, after an official tour that included visits to Ceylon, India, Nepal, Afghanistan and Pakistan, U Thant returned to New York convinced that the cessation of the bombing of North Vietnam was the way to peace.

In February 1968, in New Delhi, he met the Consul General of Hanoi, who stressed that his government would hold talks with Washington only after the cessation of the bombing and other military activities against his country. U Thant put to the Consul-General several questions to pass on to Hanoi.

On February 14, 1968, U Thant flew to Paris after he had received an urgent message from the Quai d'Orsay that Mai Van Bo, the Hanoi representative in Paris, wanted to see him.

Van Bo told him that he was authorised to declare that talks with

*Press release SG/SM/ 682 of March 28, 1967.

Washington could begin as soon as the cessation of the bombing and other acts of war against the North became effective. On his return to New York, U Thant gave a full report to Ambassador Arthur Goldberg, who, after Adlai Stevenson's sudden death, had succeeded as US representative at the UN. Goldberg had direct access to President Johnson and immediately arranged for U Thant to meet the President in Washington on February 21. On March 31, President Johnson announced that the bombing would cease except in the areas north of the demilitarised zone.

On April 3, 1968, press despatches quoted Hanoi radio as saying that North Vietnam was ready to meet American representatives to consider an end to the fighting. To keep up the peace momentum, U Thant maintained his contacts with Washington and Hanoi, and suggested Paris, Geneva or Warsaw as a possible venue for the talks. Agreement was soon reached to begin the peace talks in Paris on May 10. The talks were protracted and difficult, but five years later a preliminary agreement was reached with a new administration in Washington under Richard Nixon and with Henry Kissinger heading the US delegation in Paris.

U Thant's involvement in a plan – never realised – for Pope Paul VI to visit Vietnam in 1968 is described in the next chapter.

5

U THANT AND POPE PAUL VI

THE POPE'S VISIT TO THE GENERAL ASSEMBLY

The visit of Pope Paul VI to the United Nations on October 14, 1965, was the culmination of months of painstaking thought and preparations. It was U Thant's idea, first conceived in December 1964. To the critics and sceptics who cautioned him against issuing such an invitation without a specific mandate from the General Assembly, he said, 'No impartial observer could accuse a Buddhist Secretary-General of prejudice in inviting the Head of the Roman Catholic Church to the UN.'

The chartered Alitalia airliner in which Pope Paul travelled from the Vatican City in Rome to the international territory of the United Nations in New York touched down at John F. Kennedy International Airport at 9.30 a.m., on October 4, 1965. U Thant went aboard to greet his honoured guest and welcome him on behalf of the United Nations.

Accompanied by the Secretary-General, the Pope came down the ramp at the foot of which the UN Chief of Protocol, Pierre de Meulemeester, presented Amintore Fanfani of Italy, President of the General Assembly; Nelson A. Rockefeller, Governor of New York State; Dean Rusk, United States Secretary of State; Robert F. Wagner, Mayor of New York City; and Cardinal Francis Spellman of New York. The Secretary-General escorted Pope Paul VI over a red velvet carpet to the microphone from which the Pope addressed the dignitaries assembled to welcome him at the airport.

After these ceremonies, an official motorcade through the streets of New York City brought the Pope to St Patrick's Cathedral. There a brief service was held at noon. Later Pope Paul had a private meeting with the President of the United States, Lyndon B. Johnson, who had travelled from Washington to meet him, at the apartment of the United States Ambassador to the UN, at the Waldorf Towers.

The Pope and his party then went by motorcade to the United Nations and were met at its main entrance by the Chief of Protocol. As the Pope entered the building, he was welcomed by the Secretary-General and together they paid a short visit to the United Nations Meditation Room.

The Pope was then escorted to the ceremonial stairway which leads to the Assembly Hall, and was greeted by Amintore Fanfani, Foreign Minister of Italy and President of the General Assembly. As he entered the hall, accompanied by the President and U Thant, the assembled delegates rose and gave a standing ovation. With arms raised in acknowledgement of the greeting, the Pope walked down the aisle through the applauding audience, mounted the podium and sat in the high white chair, placed there for him, to hear the welcoming addresses of the President and the Secretary-General.

In introducing Pope Paul to the General Assembly, U Thant said: 'It is the cause of peace which brings His Holiness into our midst. It was the cause of peace – for all men on earth, without distinction as to race, religion, nationality or political belief – which led me, many months ago, to explore with His Holiness the possibility of his being present at a meeting of the General Assembly such as this, so that he might join his efforts for peace to those of the representatives of the member-states of the United Nations.

'On December 4 last, in Bombay, His Holiness voiced a special appeal, which moved me and many others deeply, as reflecting the aspirations of mankind and as being closely in keeping with the purpose and objectives of the United Nations – an appeal to all the governments of the world to undertake, in the words of His Holiness, "a peaceful battle against the sufferings of their less fortunate brothers".

'Shortly afterwards, on January 15, His Holiness entrusted to me, as Secretary-General of the United Nations, the text of his appeal. I accepted it, as an invaluable source of inspiration for me and for the Organisation which I serve. That appeal, and the desire of His Holiness to place it at the service of the United Nations, prompted me, with the full support of the then President of the General Assembly, to seek the agreement of His Holiness to appear before, and address, the General Assembly of the United Nations. That historic occasion has now arrived. It is taking place at a time when there is a renewal of confidence in our Organisation. It is a time, also, of grave dangers to the peace of the world. In expressing my deep gratitude to His Holiness, I do so in the conviction that all of us who work for the purposes of the United Nations will draw from his presence here, inspiration for our continued struggle to attain those goals of peace and human wellbeing.'

Pope Paul began his 30-minute 'colloquy with the whole world' to the assembled delegates at 3.35 p.m. It was delivered in French, and the following is extracted from the condensed version of the text in English provided by the Vatican:

'As we begin our address to this audience, unique in the world, we wish first to express Our profound gratitude to Mr Thant, your Secretary-General, for the invitation which he extended to Us to visit the United Nations on the occasion of the twentieth anniversary of this world institution for peace and co-operation among the peoples of all the earth.

'You are all well aware that this meeting between us is of a twofold nature; it bears the stamp both of simplicity and of grandeur. Simplicity, because he who speaks to you is a man like you; he is your brother, and even one of the least among you, representing as you do sovereign states. He has not temporal power, no ambition to compete with you. In point of fact, We have nothing to ask for, no questions to raise.

'You all know who We are. Whatever your opinion of the Roman Pontiff, you know Our mission: We are the bearer of a message for all mankind. This We are, not only in Our own name and in the name of the great Catholic family, but also in the name of those Christian brethren who share the feelings We express here. We have been on the way for a long time and We bear with Us a long history; here We celebrate the end of a laborious pilgrimage in search of a colloquy with the whole world, a pilgrimage which began when We were given the command: "Go and bring the good news to all nations." And it is you who represent all nations.

'We wish Our message to be a moral and solemn ratification of this high Institution. The message comes of Our experience of history.

'We are aware that We are making Our own, the voices both of the dead and of the living; of the dead who fell in the terrible wars of the past while dreaming of harmony and world peace; of the living who survived war and already in their hearts condemn those who would try to bring it again; the young generations of today going forward confidently in rightful expectation of a better humanity. We also make Our own the voice of the poor, the disinherited, the unfortunate; of those who yearn for justice, for the dignity of life, for freedom, for wellbeing and for progress. The peoples turn to the United Nations as to the ultimate hope for harmony and peace. The building you have made must never again fall in ruins; it must be perfected and conformed to the demands world history will make. You mark a stage in the development of mankind: henceforth no turning back, you must go forward.

'To the majority of States, no longer able to ignore each other, you offer an extremely simple and fruitful form of co-existence. You do not, of course, confer existence upon States, but you qualify each nation as worthy to sit in the ordered assembly of the peoples; you grant to each national sovereign community a recognition of high moral and juridical value, and you guarantee it an honourable international citizenship. This in itself is a great service to the cause of mankind: clearly to define and to honour the national entities of the world community and to establish them in a juridical status which entitles them to be recognised and respected by all, and from which there may derive an ordered and stable system of international life.

'And allow Us to congratulate you on having had the wisdom to leave the door to this Assembly open to the young peoples, to the states which have but lately attained national independence and freedom; their presence here is proof of the universality and magnanimity which inform the principles of this Institution.

'Your Charter goes even further; and Our message goes forward with it. You exist and work to unite the nations, to associate the states together. Let Us use the formula: to bring together one and another. You are an Association. You are a bridge between the peoples. You are a network of relations among the states.

'Go forward. We shall say more: strive to bring back among you any who may have left you; consider means of calling into your pact of brotherhood, in honour and loyalty, those who do not yet share in it. Act so that those still outside will desire and deserve the confidence of all; and then be generous in granting it. Let no one, as a member of your Association, be superior to the others: not one above another. This is the formula of equality. We well know that there are other factors to be considered besides that of mere membership of this body. But equality, too, is a part of its constitution.

'And here Our message reaches its highest point. Never again one against another, never, never again! Is it not to this end above all that the United Nations was born: against war and for peace? Listen to the lucid words of a great man now departed, John Kennedy, who declared four years ago: "Mankind must put an end to war, or war will put an end to mankind." The blood of millions of men, countless and unheard-of sufferings, useless massacres and fearful ruins have sealed the pact uniting you with a vow which must change the future history of the world: never again war, war never again! Peace, it is peace, which must guide the destiny of the peoples and of all mankind!

'Thanks to you and glory to you for the conflicts you have prevented and for those you have settled. The results of your efforts for peace, up to these last days, even if not yet decisive, deserve that We venture to interpret the feelings of the whole world and in its name express to you both congratulations and gratitude.

'Peace, as you know, is built not only by means of politics and the balance of forces and interests. It is built with the spirit, with ideas, with works of peace. You are labouring at this great work. But you are as yet only at the beginning of your labours. Will the world ever succeed in changing the exclusive and bellicose state of mind which up to now has woven so much of its history?

'If you wish to be brothers, let the weapons fall from your hands. You cannot love with offensive weapons in your hands. Even before they cause victims and ruins, weapons, especially the terrible weapons modern science has given you, beget bad dreams, nourish bad feelings, create nightmares, mistrust and sombre resolves; they exact enormous expenditures; they bring to a halt projects of useful work undertaken in solidarity; they warp the psychology of peoples.

'Many among you looked with favour upon the invitation in the cause of peace that We addressed to all states from Bombay last December; to devote to the benefit of the developing countries at least part of the savings which can be realised by reducing armaments. We here renew that invitation.

'You are not satisfied with making co-existence between nations easier; you are organising brotherly co-operation among the peoples. Here a system of solidarity is being set up, so that the high aims of civilised order may win the unanimous and ordered support of the whole family of peoples, to the good of all and everyone.

'This is what is most beautiful in the United Nations; this is its most truly human face; this is the ideal which mankind dreams of on its pilgrimage through time; this is the world's greatest hope.

'What you proclaim here are the fundamental rights and duties of man, his dignity, his freedom, and above all his religious freedom. But it is not enough to feed the starving; each man must also be assured of a life consistent with his dignity. And this is what you are striving to achieve.

'We know how ardently you work to conquer illiteracy and to spread culture throughout the world: to give men proper and modern medical assistance; to put at man's service the marvellous resources of science and of the technique of organisation.

'We Ourselves would also like to set an example. We wish to intensify the efforts of Our charitable institutions against the world's hunger and to meet its chief needs. It is thus, and in no other way, that peace is built.

'One word more, this edifice you are building does not rest upon purely material and earthly foundations, for it would then be a house built on sand; above all, it rests on our consciences. Yes! the moment of "conversion" has come, of personal transformation, of inner renewal.

'Now the hour for a halt is upon us. Never before has there been such a need for an appeal to the moral conscience of man as there is today, in an era marked by such human progress. For the peril comes neither from progress nor from science; on the contrary, properly used, they could resolve many of the grave problems which beset mankind. The real peril is in man, who has at hand ever more powerful instruments, suited as much to destruction as to the highest conquests. The edifice of modern civilisation must be built on spiritual principles, which alone can not only support it. And it is Our conviction, that these indispensable principles of higher wisdom can rest only on faith in God. To us in any case, and to all those who receive the ineffable revelation which Christ has given us of Him, He is the living God, the father of all men.'

When the Pope completed his speech, he added in a vigorous voice the words '*Jamais plus la guerre!*' and repeated them twice – they had not been included in the official text. At that heartfelt cry, the audience of more than 4,000 people, deeply moved, rose in a standing ovation that lasted ten minutes.

After his address and the cheering were over, the Pope, still escorted by the President of the General Assembly and the Secretary-General, visited the three main Council Chambers. He spoke to some 500 representatives of information media gathered in the room where normally the Economic and Social Council holds its meetings. Then he was escorted to the North Lounge overlooking the UN gardens on the East River, where the Secretary-General gave an official reception in his honour. More than 500 prominent personalities were presented.

The Pope also met, separately, Luis Vidal Zaglio, the Uruguayan Minister for External Relations, President of the Security Council; Maurice Couve de Murville, the French Foreign Minister; Andrei Gromyko, the Soviet Foreign Minister; Michael Stewart, the British Foreign Secretary; and Dean Rusk, United States Secretary of State. Another, smaller reception by the Secretary-General in the Pope's honour followed on the thirty-eighth floor of the Secretariat building – the floor where the Secretary-General has his offices. Before leaving there, Pope Paul had a private meeting with U Thant in the Secretary-General's office. The Pope presented the Secretary-General with his official gifts to the Organisation – a painting, 'Christ Crucified', by Georges Rouault; a diamond cross and a diamond ring, which the Pope suggested be sold to 'help the poor of the world'.

At 11.30 on the night of October 4, after he had celebrated an open-air mass for peace, the Pope left New York for Rome. In all, Pope Paul VI spent three hours at United Nations Headquarters. He was seen and heard in the halls and chambers of the Organisation by some 7,000 people. Millions more, in all parts of the world, heard him on radio and saw him on television as he delivered his message of peace.*

Yet others followed the event through the reports sent out by more than 1,500 representatives of the information media – the largest number of correspondents ever to gather at the United Nations.

AN UNPUBLISHED PAGE OF HISTORY

U Thant was elated by the Pope's visit. He repeated over and over that the Foreign Ministers of the Permanent Members of the Security Council, including Gromyko, had had separate meetings with the Pope, at their own request. The warm welcome, and especially the standing ovation from delegates representing millions of people of different races, religions and political ideologies in the UN General Assembly had been particularly gratifying to the Secretary-General, and gave further inspiration to his tolerant and open-minded nature.

In his private discussions with the Pope on that occasion, U Thant dwelt at length on the Vietnam war. He spoke passionately of the sufferings of the Vietnamese people in both North and South, and reiterated his conviction that military measures could never resolve the conflict.

In 1982, Monsignor Alberto Giovannetti, who had been the permanent observer of the Holy See at the United Nations in the 1960s, revealed to me that U Thant's plea had made a deep impression on Pope Paul. It influenced his decision, in 1968, to plan a visit to the two Vietnams and his subsequent request to U Thant to contact Hanoi. Both Pope Paul and U Thant were discreet. The projected visit did not materialise, and the episode has remained buried until the writing of these pages.

It was on Monday, July 29, 1968, that Monsignor Paul Marcinkus (later, as an Archbishop, to play a prominent role close to Pope John Paul II) came to see U Thant conveying a message from Pope Paul. It stated the Pope's intention to visit Vietnam, both North and South, immediately after the Ecumenical Council in Colombia, scheduled to take place

*Never Again War, OPI official publication, New York, 1965.

on August 22–25. In the message, the Pope explained that he planned to do this in order to demonstrate his interest in, and admiration for, the entire Vietnamese people.

The same day, U Thant sent for Roger Chayet, the French Chargé d'Affaires (in the absence of Ambassador Armand Bérard), and handed him an aide-memoire containing a summary of the Pope's written statement. U Thant asked Chayet to transmit the aide-memoire immediately to Michel Debré, the Foreign Minister, with the request that it be conveyed to Mai Van Bo, Delegate General of North Vietnam, in Paris.

On Wednesday, July 31, Chayet saw U Thant and told him that his Foreign Minister wanted to know if it would not be possible for the Pope to send the request through his own representative in Paris directly to Mai Van Bo. U Thant explained that the Pope did not want anybody to know about his plans at that stage, and this was the reason why he had asked for U Thant's good offices.

On Thursday, August 1, Monsignor Marcinkus saw U Thant and asked if the Pope's message had been transmitted. U Thant mentioned the delay that had been caused by the query from the French Foreign Minister. On August 2, Chayet informed U Thant that Foreign Minister Debré had personally transmitted the message to Mai Van Bo, that same day. Then the following Tuesday, August 6, Marcinkus saw U Thant and was told by him that the Pope's message had been delivered. Marcinkus told U Thant that he had been to Washington over the weekend and seen President Johnson and the Secretary of State, Dean Rusk. On instructions from the Vatican, Marcinkus informed them of the Pope's intention to visit both North Vietnam and South Vietnam, and that the Pope had sent a message to U Thant for transmission to Hanoi. Marcinkus added that both the President and the Secretary of State were glad to know of the Pope's plans, and that U Thant was acting as an intermediary with Hanoi. Marcinkus told U Thant that the Pope might decide to go to Saigon alone if Hanoi's reply were negative.

On August 9, Ambassador Bérard of France saw U Thant and told him that no reply had yet been received from Hanoi. On August 12, Marcinkus telephoned U Thant from Rome to say that the Pope wanted to finalise his travel plans before August 16. It was his intention to proceed to Hanoi directly from Colombia on August 25, so that he could reach Hanoi the next day. The Pope would very much appreciate if U Thant could send a reminder to Hanoi so that a reply would be received before August 16. U Thant saw Ambassador Bérard the same day and requested that Foreign Minister Debré ask Mai Van Bo to expedite the reply from Hanoi.

On August 13, Bérard saw U Thant and gave him the reply which was signed by President Ho Chi Minh and addressed to Foreign Minister Debré. It read: 'President Ho Chi Minh expresses his sincere thanks to His Holiness for his concern for the problem of restoring peace in Vietnam and his intention of going to Hanoi in order to demonstrate his admiration for the Vietnamese people.

'Unfortunately, on account of the war, the required conditions for welcoming His Holiness to the Democratic Republic of Vietnam do not exist, and this is very regrettable.

'The war in Vietnam is due to the aggression of the United States. Should the United States put an end to that aggression, peace will be immediately restored.

'President Ho Chi Minh expresses the hope that His Holiness, in the name of humanity and justice, will use his high authority to demand that the United States government respect the fundamental national rights of the Vietnamese people in accordance with the Geneva agreements of 1954. The President conveys to His Holiness his compliments and best wishes of good health.'

U Thant sent the text of Ho Chi Minh's reply (in French, with an English translation) to Monsignor Marcinkus at the Vatican on the evening of August 13. Earlier in the day, he had sent a cable to Marcinkus about the method of despatch of the message and called him by telephone. Marcinkus promised to keep U Thant posted on the Pope's decision.

Pope Paul subsequently sent U Thant a signed letter thanking him for his collaboration and saying that after considering the letter of President Ho Chi Minh, he had decided not to go to South Vietnam, 'lest such a gesture have an adverse effect on the quest for peace which we and the world so ardently desire, or even aggravate the situation'.

On the following pages are:
(pages 65–8)   U Thant's record of the meeting with Mgr Marcinkus referred to on page 62, and its consequences; (page 69) his aide-memoire to Roger Chayet referred to on page 63; and (pages 70–1) Pope Paul's letter to U Thant, announcing his abandonment of the project.

(B)

Passed on to c.d.a. of
France for transmission.

Ihan
29/7

<u>T O P   S E C R E T</u>

29 July 1968

1. The Holy Father would most ardently desire to visit Hanoi and aigon, immediately after the International Eucharistic Congress in olombia (August 22-25).

2. To give a new public testimony of His particular interest in nd of His admiration of the entire Vietnamese people.

3. To meet briefly, after having greeted the civil authorities, ith the Vietnamese Catholic communities. (This does not exclude other eetings with local humanitarian organizations.)

4. The Holy Father plans to arrive in Hanoi, accompanied by a very estricted number of people, his plane to take off from a neutral country, epending on technical possibilities. He will remain in Hanoi only for a ort time.

5. The Holy Father wishes to underline that His projected visit to ietnam does not have any political intent or significance, but rather only pastoral and humanitarian purpose, one of consideration and sympathy for e Vietnamese people.

6. No desire to interfere in any way with Paris talks. But the Pope ll, naturally, be disposed to hear whatever President Ho Chi Minh or her leaders in Hanoi would communicate to Him.

7. He is asking U Thant to transmit this to Hanoi.

8. Please reply as soon as possible.

TOP SECRET

THE POPE'S PROJECTED VISIT TO VIET-NAM

On Monday, 29 July 1968, Monsignor Marcinkus saw me and conveyed to me the Pope's message regarding his intention to visit Viet-Nam (both North and South) immediately after the Ecumenical Council in Colombia which takes place from 22 to 25 August. He left with me a short statement outlining the Pope's intentions and programme (A).

On the same day I sent for the Chargé d'Affaires of France (Chayet) and explained to him the Pope's message and handed over to him a summary of the Pope's written statement (B). I asked Mr. Chayet to transmit this immediately to his Foreign Minister with my request to transmit this to Mr. Mai Van Bo, Delegate-General of North Viet-Nam in Paris, as soon as possible.

On Wednesday, 31 July, Mr. Chayet saw me again and told me that his Foreign Minister wanted to know if it would not be possible for the Pope to transmit the request through his (the Pope's) representative in Paris directly to Mr. Mai Van Bo. I explained to him that the Pope did not want anybody to know about his plans at this stage and that was the reason why he was asking for my good offices. I reiterated my request that the message be conveyed to Mr. Mai Van Bo by the French Foreign Minister.

On Thursday, 1 August, Monsignor Marcinkus saw me and asked me if the Pope's message had been transmitted. I explained to him about the query of the French Foreign Minister yesterday.

On Friday, 2 August, Mr. Chayet saw me and informed me that the Pope's message had been transmitted today (Friday) by his Foreign Minister directly to Mr. Mai Van Bo.

On Tuesday, 6 August, Monsignor Marcinkus saw me again and asked me if the message had been delivered. I explained to him that the French Foreign Minister personally delivered the message to Mr. Mai Van Bo on 2 August. Marcinkus told me he went down to Washington over the weekend and on Monday he saw President Johnson and Secretary of State Dean Rusk and informed them of the Pope's intention to visit both North Viet-Nam and South Viet-Nam and that the Pope had sent a message to U Thant for

- 2 -

Visit of Pope

transmission to Hanoi. According to Monsignor Marcinkus both the
President and the Secretary of State were glad to know the Pope's
plans and they were glad that U Thant was acting as an intermediary
between the Pope and Hanoi. Marcinkus told me that the Pope might
decide to go to Saigon even if Hanoi's reply is negative.

On Friday, 9 August, Ambassador Bérard saw me and told me that
no reply had yet been received from Hanoi. On Monday, 12 August,
Monsignor Marcinkus telephoned me from Rome and informed me that the
Pope wanted to finalize his travel plans before Friday, 16 August.
It was his intention to proceed to Hanoi directly from Colombia on
25 August so that he could reach Hanoi on 26 August. He would very
much appreciate if I could send a reminder to Hanoi to get a reply
before Friday. I saw Ambassador Bérard the same day and transmitted
Marcinkus' message with the request that his Foreign Minister please

ask Mr. Mai Van Bo to expedite the reply from Hanoi so that I could receive it if possible before Friday.

On Tuesday, 13 August, Ambassador Bérard saw me and gave me the reply which was signed by President Ho Chi Minh addressed to Foreign Minister Debré (C). The Foreign Minister received it on Monday, 12 August, before he received Mr. Bérard's message from me which was transmitted to Paris on Monday night. The text of Ho Chi Minh's reply together with an English translation were sent to Monsignor Marcinkus by pouch through the United Nations Information Centre in Rome in the evening of Tuesday, 13 August. I sent a cable to Marcinkus earlier in the day about the pouching of the message and I talked to him on the telephone at 5 p.m. on the same day. Marcinkus told me that he would keep me posted with the Pope's decision as soon as possible.

To His Excellency

U THANT

Secretary-General of the United Nations

We take this first occasion, after receiving Your Excellency's gracious reply, to express Our sincere thanks for your prompt collaboration in a matter so dear to Us.

Having considered the letter of President Ho Chi Minh, We have decided not to go to South Vietnam, lest such a gesture have an adverse effect on the quest for peace which We and the world so ardently desire, or even aggravate the situation. We further fear that possible hostile acts, occurring on the occasion of such a visit, might be wrongly interpreted, and might even be the cause of much sorrow to an already tried population.

Our desire to do all in Our power to hasten a just and equitable solution to the war that afflicts that suffering part of the world has not been lessened by the negative response; the response has rather heightened Our determination to do whatever is possible in order to reach a peaceful solution.

We request Your Excellency to be so kind as to have transmitted to President Ho Chi Minh the enclosed note addressed to him.

We deeply appreciate your valued assistance, and We ask God to bless your constant efforts in the cause of peace.

From the Vatican, August 18th, 1968

Paulus P.P. VI

6

NASSER ORDERS THE WITHDRAWAL
OF U.N.E.F.

It was late afternoon on May 16, 1967. William Powell, the UN spokesman, and I were in Brian Urquhart's office on the thirty-eighth floor of the UN building when Beatrice, his Chinese secretary, came in with a folder. She gave it to him without a word. Urquhart opened the folder, had a quick look at it, and jumped to his feet with the words: 'I must go and see Ralph.'

Minutes later, Ralph Bunche and Urquhart rushed across the corridor to the Secretary-General's office to confer with U Thant. That folder carried a cryptic message from General Rikhye, Commander of UNEF, that General Mohammed Fawzi, chief of staff of the United Arab Republic (or UAR, as Egypt was called then), had asked for the withdrawal of all UN troops from observer posts along the borders. U Thant immediately cabled back telling Rikhye to await further orders.

The same evening, U Thant requested Ambassador Mohammed Awad El Kony, the UAR's permanent representative to the United Nations, to come and see him. El Kony had not received any news from Cairo, but promised to check and report back.

Livio Zeno Zencovich, the scholarly Italian diplomat who was Director of the United Nations Information Centre in Cairo from 1967 to 1971, wrote in an essay which he entitled 'President Nasser, as seen between the Six-Day War of June 1967 and his death in September 1970 – A Personal Memoire':*

'It was ten o'clock at night, Cairo time, on 16 May 1967, when Brigadier Mokhtar handed General Rikhye, in Gaza, the following communication signed by the Chief of Staff of the UAR Armed Forces:

"To your information. I gave my instructions to all UAR Armed Forces to be ready for action against Israel the moment it might carry out any aggressive action against any Arab country. Due to these instructions, our troops are already concentrated in Sinai on our Eastern borders. For the sake of complete secure [sic] of all UN troops which install observation posts along our border, I request that you issue your orders to withdraw all these troops immediately. I have given my

*Unpublished. Original in Archives of UN Library, Palais des Nations, Geneva.

72

instructions to our Commander of the eastern zone concerning this subject. Inform back the fulfilment of this request. Yours, *Ferik Awal**
M. Fawzi.''

'Brigadier Mokhtar did not confine himself to the delivery of this written communication. Verbally, he requested General Rikhye to order the immediate withdrawal of the United Nations (Yugoslav) garrisons from El Sabha (in Sinai) and Sharm el Sheikh, since UAR armed forces must gain control of these two places on that very night; and it was already ten p.m. The UNEF Commander, quite properly, replied that he did not have the authority to withdraw UN troops from these positions on such an order and could do so only on instructions from the Secretary-General. To the latter, he immediately cabled this astonishing development. It was the first intimation of the Egyptian decision.

'At this point one question becomes relevant. If the Syrians, for whose sake the withdrawal of UNEF was alleged to have been requested, had no advance notion of it; if the Jordanians, whose security and integrity were to be so gravely jeopardised, knew nothing about it; if the Secretary-General himself, who was the only proper channel for such a request, was kept in the dark; who then in Egypt, and particularly in Nasser's own entourage, knew?

'According to well-informed Egyptian sources, it is to be ruled out that neither Dr Mahmoud Fawzi, then holding the title of Presidential Adviser on Foreign Affairs, nor the Foreign Minister, Mahmoud Riad, nor even the Prime Minister, Sidky Suleiman were informed, let alone consulted. All military sources would confirm that the links between President Nasser and the Armed Forces were so exclusive as to have made the by-passing of the Prime Minister and of the whole government machinery an established practice. Even in matters of their own functional competence, the civilian authorities were often ignored. Under these circumstances, it was not to be wondered at if, less than three hours after Brigadier Mokhtar's communication, the Permanent Representative of the UAR in New York, Ambassador El Kony, summoned by the Secretary-General, gave the impression 'of not having been kept in the picture'.

'Surprising as this might seem, the Egyptian Foreign Minister, in Cairo, learnt of the decision taken by his Head of State from New York, from U Thant. Even more surprising, and in itself an enormity considering

---

Ferik Awal, Arabic for Gen. Fawzi's military rank.

Dr Fawzi's role in the setting-up of UNEF, was the latter's exclusion from this vital question; a fact which fitted, however, into the pattern of the decision-taking process in the UAR at the highest level.

'An equally unexpected conclusion, supported by reliable evidence, was that even Zakaria Mohieddine, who was holding at that time the title of Vice-President of the Republic, and to whom Nasser was to entrust very soon exceptional responsibilities, was not in the know.

Did Mohammed Hassanein Heikal participate in the decision? His relationship with the President was of such a nature that he generally showed awareness of the most exclusive military secrets – his having been left completely in the dark on this occasion was described as 'unthinkable'. But that he was consulted was less likely.

'Who knew? It was in the late afternoon of May 16, that Marshal Amer, Minister of War and Commander in Chief, telephoned, in person, the Office of Operations of the UAR General Staff, to intimate that Brigadier Mokhtar was airborne, on his way to El Arish, to demand from General Rikhye the withdrawal of UNEF. The Marshal ordered the Chief of Operations to take all the necessary measures for the follow-up to the withdrawal, some of which were to take place that very night. For the General Staff this was a surprise. When the question of the re-occupation of Sharm el Sheik was considered for action, it was referred to a ranking officer, General Nofal, who knew everything about the place for having served there and who understood the military as well as the political implications of such a re-occupation. What orders were to be given to the Egyptian garrison in the event of Israeli ships sailing past the island? This raised problems of gunnery, of armament, of ammunition, of supplies. These complex matters having been examined in the Office of Operations, it was decided that General Nofal himself should phone the Field Marshal, submit to him his queries, and clarify with him the orders which were to be issued.

'When the intricacies of the situation dawned upon Marshal Amer, he realised that time was needed to sort them out. By then, however, Brig. Mokhtar was about to reach his destination. The Field Marshal instructed therefore the Office of Operations to issue orders to intercept him and to request him to await further communications; but when this signal had reached its destination, Brigadier Mokhtar was already on the road to General Rikhye's headquarters and it was too late to reach him.

'Thus General Fawzi's message was delivered amidst misgivings and counter orders, and UNEF's fate was sealed.

'Until the despatch of Brigadier Mokhtar, knowledge of the decision

Above, U Thant taking the oath of office on his appointment as Acting Secretary-General in the presence of Mongi Slim, President of the General Assembly, November 1961. *Below*, in conversation with Trygve Lie, first UN Secretary-General, April 1964.

Above, with Chairman Nikita S. Khrushchev, Yalta, August 1962. *Below*, with President Leopold S. Senghor of Senegal, Dakar, January 1970.

Above, with (*from left*) General I.J. Rikhye, Omar Loutfi, G. Amachree and C.V. Narasimhan, November 1962. *Below*, being welcomed by Ramses Nassif on returning to UN Headquarters after a long illness, December 6, 1971.

Above, introducing Ralph Bunche to President John F. Kennedy at UN Headquarters, September 1963. *Below*, guest of honour at a banquet in the White House, Washington, August 1964, with President Lyndon B. Johnson and, *behind*, Mrs Johnson.

In Cairo, May 1967, with (*from left*) the Egyptian Foreign Minister Riad, President Nasser, General Rikhye (Commander, UNEF) and Dr Fawzi (Presidential Adviser on Foreign Affairs).

Above, with Pope Paul VI at UN Headquarters, October 4, 1965. *Below*, receiving the honorary degree of LL.D. from Dr Frederick Boland, Chancellor of Trinity College, Dublin (and former UN Ambassador), July 12, 1968.

Above, congratulating Dr Kurt Waldheim on his appointment as UN Secretary-General, December 21, 1971. *Below*, receiving the credentials of Javier Perez de Cuellar (UN Secretary-General, 1981–) on the latter's appointment as Permanent Representative of Peru to the UN, February 1971.

Above, with Vice-President Richard Nixon and Mrs Patricia Nixon in Rangoon, November 1953. *Below*, with (*left*) his mother Daw Nan Thaung and (*right*) his wife Daw Thien Tin at a monastery in Rangoon, February 1967.

Above, with (*from left*) his son-in-law Tyn Myint U, his wife Daw Thien Tin holding their second grandson, his grandson Ko Ko and his daughter Aye Aye. *Below*, holding Ko Ko, who was born a year after the death of Maung Tin Maung, U Thant's only son.

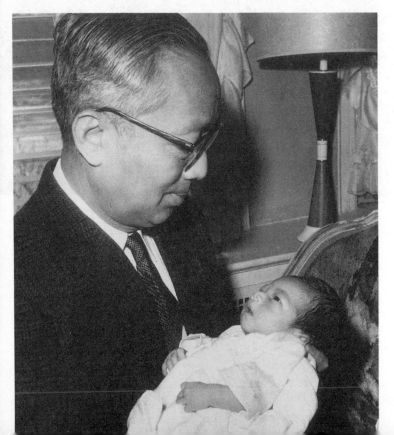

The mausoleum containing U Thant's remains, near the magnificent Shwe Dagon pagoda, Rangoon. In 1987, when this picture was taken, it was in a state of sad neglect. (Photo: *Asiaweek*)

was confined, therefore, to four persons: President Nasser, Marshal Amer, General Fawzi and General Mortagui, currently described as 'the Commander of the Front'. Considering the total black-out of the UAR General Staff until then, the inferential conclusion seemed justified that both General Fawzi and General Mortagui were put in the picture at the last moment because of the time that was necessary for drafting the communication and instructing its bearer; but the decision itself, one should assume, was discussed by the top leaders only and reached by them alone without outside intervention or advice.'

The confusion in Egypt during the fateful decision was described by Dr Fawzi a year later as 'gross miscalculations based on gross misinformation'.

Back in New York, on May 17 U Thant, accompanied by Ralph Bunche and Brian Urquhart, met the representatives of the countries providing contingents to UNEF (Brazil, Canada, Denmark, India, Norway, Sweden and Yugoslavia). The Secretary-General told them that if a formal request for the withdrawal were received from the government of the UAR, he would have to comply since UNEF was stationed on Egyptian territory only with the consent of the government. He said that the situation in the Middle East was extremely serious, and because the withdrawal would aggravate it, he intended to appeal to Cairo to reconsider its decision.

U Thant then met Ambassador El Kony and gave him an aide-memoire indicating that the request made by General Fawzi to General Rikhye was wrong in procedure. Such a request should come from the government to the Secretary-General. The aide-memoire asked Cairo to clarify its intentions. If withdrawal meant a temporary one from the armistice lines, this was unacceptable. If complete withdrawal was the intention, the Secretary-General pointed out the dangerous consequences of such action, but added that he would have no choice but to comply and order the withdrawal. (UNEF had originally been stationed on Egyptian territory, with Egypt's consent, after an agreement between President Nasser and Secretary-General Dag Hammarskjöld in 1956.)

Throughout this critical time, U Thant depended heavily on the advice of Ralph Bunche, whom he considered the top authority on the Middle East. As Secretary-General, U Thant travelled extensively in Asia, Europe, Africa and Latin America, but he never visited any country in the Middle East except when he briefly passed through Cairo in 1964 to address an African Summit there. The complex mixture of history, prejudice, aspirations and paranoia that have always governed Middle East politics eluded him.

On May 18, U Thant met Ambassador Gideon Rafael of Israel, who argued against the withdrawal of UNEF. U Thant asked whether if there were an official request for a withdrawal of UNEF from Egypt, Israel would agree to UNEF being stationed on the Israeli side of the armistice line. Ambassador Rafael rejected this idea out of hand.

An hour later, Ambassador El Kony came to see U Thant. In the outer office, El Kony took me aside to say he was going to hand U Thant the formal request for the withdrawal. He had been on the telephone to Cairo, talking to Mahmoud Riad, the Foreign Minister. He said that the atmosphere in Egypt was very tense. The government feared that certain countries were trying to put pressure on U Thant not to withdraw UNEF. Foreign Minister Riad, he continued, was so incensed that if the worst came to the worst, UNEF would be disarmed and shipped in trucks out of Egypt. El Kony, whom I had known for many years, was an extremely honest diplomat – too honest to be a politician! I listened quietly, and said: 'I am sure you are not going to tell U Thant all that!'

El Kony then entered U Thant's office and Ralph Bunche joined them. In receiving the formal request for the withdrawal, U Thant warned El Kony of the dangerous consequences that would follow from it, and added that before issuing the withdrawal order, he intended to send an urgent appeal to President Nasser to reconsider. El Kony urged him to delay the appeal until he had discussed it with the Foreign Minister. In the evening, El Kony came again to tell U Thant that Riad had advised against it and stressed that such an appeal would be rebuffed. At that point, U Thant raised the question of going to Cairo and El Kony immediately responded that his government would welcome such a visit.

After the meeting, U Thant briefed me on what transpired. We were alone, and when he finished I told him I felt strongly that he should send his appeal anyway. I said that perhaps President Nasser had put himself in a corner, and the appeal would give him a graceful way out. I reminded U Thant of his appeal to Khrushchev and Kennedy during the missile crisis in 1962, and how he had cabled it without any consultations with the Soviet and American Ambassadors to the United Nations. Out of my respect and affection for the man, I stopped short of telling him it had been a mistake, in the first place, to consult El Kony about the appeal.

Patiently, he listened to me and ended the conversation by saying that

Ralphe Bunche took a different view and had now advised against the appeal. He added that I should get ready to leave with him for Cairo, and instructed me to enquire discreetly from El Kony whether there would be any objection to our taking along on the trip Lucien Lemieux, his Canadian secretary. There were rumblings in Cairo against Canada, with rumours flying that Ottawa was against pulling out the Canadian contingent which made up an important part of UNEF. However, El Kony said that anyone in U Thant's party was welcome.

On May 19, before departing for Egypt, U Thant submitted a report to the Security Council on the crisis. He said: 'I do not wish to be alarmist, but I cannot avoid the warning to the Council that in my view the current situation in the Near East is more disturbing, indeed, more menacing than at any time since the fall of 1956.'

U Thant, Donald Thomas, his security officer, Lucien Lemieux the private secretary, and I left by Air France on the evening of May 22, and arrived the next morning (May 23) at Orly airport in Paris. We were met by G. Lacharière of the Quay d'Orsay and Gibson Parker, director of the UN Information Centre in Paris. Glumly they told U Thant the news that President Nasser had announced the closure of the Strait of Tiran to Israeli shipping. U Thant was shocked, but managed not to show it. He told us that war was now inevitable, and in a discreet way sought our opinion as to whether he should continue with the journey. I said that he should proceed to Cairo because if he cancelled the journey and returned to New York, it would be tantamount to inviting the antagonists to fight it out. Lacharière and Gibson Parker remained silent. He then asked us to leave him alone and I knew he was going to meditate before taking his decision, as he always did. When we joined him again after a few minutes, he had made up his mind to go to Cairo.

We landed at Cairo airport at 17.00 hours Cairo time, on May 23. Foreign Minister Riad; General Odd Bull, Chief of Staff of UNTSO (United Nations Truce Supervisory Organisation); General Rikhye, Commander of UNEF; Laurence Michelmore, Commissioner General of UNRWA (United Nations Relief and Work Agency, which took care of the Palestine refugees), and scores of journalists were at the airport to meet us.

Following instructions, I told the correspondents that the Secretary-General did not wish to make any statement other than that he was in Cairo for urgent talks with the government about the serious situation in the Middle East.

We drove to the Nile Hilton hotel, where we stayed as guests of the government. U Thant invited the UN party to a small working dinner in his suite. I excused myself and asked his permission to use one of the official cars put at our disposal to take me to Heliopolis, a suburb to the south of Cairo, to visit my ailing mother, promising to be back immediately after dinner. He agreed.

When I returned to the hotel, I went to see him. After enquiring about my mother, he asked if I had heard about the demonstration on the bridge (Kasr El Nil bridge on the Nile, about 600 metres from the Hilton). I said I had not, but would find out. I went down to the hotel reception desk and enquired. I was told that fifty to sixty young men, presumed to be members of the Socialist Union (Nasser's party), had assembled over the bridge and were shouting 'glory to Egypt . . . we want war'. No one took them seriously, but whoever staged that demonstration showed bad taste and a complete lack of political judgement. At a time when the government claimed that Egypt had been compelled to request the withdrawal of UNEF because of Israeli threats to Syria, and President Nasser having said that Israel was concentrating thirteen brigades on the Syrian border, here in Cairo demonstrators were calling for war!

I fully reported what I had been told. U Thant listened, shook his head in disbelief, and asked if the press would publish news about the demonstration. I said that I did not think the censors would allow its publication. He commented: 'I should conclude that it was staged for my benefit!' I said that he might wish to mention the unfortunate episode to the Foreign Minister, whom he was seeing the next morning.

I also told him that I was doing my best to avoid saying anything of substance to the press, but it was very difficult. He was sympathetic but instructed me to continue my silence. I suggested that a private chat with Mohammed Hassanein Heikal, editor of *Al Ahram* and President Nasser's closest confidant, might be helpful. U Thant replied that he had heard of Heikal and was aware of his importance, but as Secretary-General he had constraints and must confine his talks to the Foreign Minister and the President. He agreed, however, to see Heikal after those talks, on the eve of his departure from Cairo.

On the morning of May 24, U Thant, accompanied by Rikhye, had a long meeting with Foreign Minister Riad which lasted until lunchtime. Before the start of this formal meeting, U Thant asked why the Strait of Tiran had been closed while he was en route to Cairo. Riad dodged the question, saying that the President would personally explain that at dinner. At the meeting, Riad went to great length to explain the reasons that prompted his government to request the withdrawal of UNEF insisting that there was an escalation of military pressure by Israel against Jordan and Syria. U Thant suggested a freeze on the situation in the Gulf of Aqaba for two to three weeks, similar to the one he had put forward in 1962 during the Cuban missile crisis. Egypt should not take any action in the Gulf, he argued, and he would appeal to Israel not to send ships during that period so as to allow time for discussions. The Foreign Minister was non committal.

After the talks, we were driven to the Tahrir (liberation) Club in downtown Cairo, a picturesque old building where we attended a luncheon given by the Foreign Minister in honour of U Thant. The elaborate menu, the beautiful room and the meticulous service contrasted sharply with the atmosphere of tension prevailing throughout the city.

In the evening, U Thant attended a dinner given by President Nasser at his residence.* Mahmoud Fawzi, adviser to the President for foreign affairs, Riad and General Rikhye attended. U Thant again expressed his surprise that the decision to close the Gulf was taken while he was on his way to Cairo, and stressed the seriousness of that action. Nasser explained that the decision had been taken a long time before but he had to announce it before U Thant's arrival so that it would not appear as a snub.

U Thant asked for Nasser's reaction to his proposal for a moratorium in the Gulf and the appointment of a special representative of the Secretary-General. Nasser said that he would accept for two weeks, provided Israel also complied. Nasser expressed his gratitude to UNEF for keeping the peace in the area and offered it the highest military decoration in recognition of its efforts, a far cry from the earlier hysterical criticism. Before leaving President Nasser, U Thant asked for, and received, a pledge that UAR military forces would not be the first to attack.

Back at the hotel, U Thant sent a coded cable to Bunche on the results of his talks, and asked him to ascertain Israel's reaction to the moratorium proposal. On the morning of May 25, Heikal came to see me at the hotel. I took him to see U Thant in his suite next door. It was a hurried conversation which lasted for no more than ten minutes. Heikal said that he would do everything to help U Thant's efforts for peace. U Thant listened, thanked him and said he had made proposals to President

*Summary record of U Thant's talks with Nasser, as corrected by U Thant, appear on the pages following this chapter.

Nasser, who had reacted sympathetically. Seeing Heikal off, I told him how pessimistic I felt after the closure of the Gulf of Aqaba, and that U Thant feared that war was inevitable and that Israel was not bluffing. Heikal assured me that the Egyptian armed forces were prepared for all eventualities.

We left Cairo on May 25, and reached New York late that night. Egypt Air was ordered to bump four first-class passengers at Cairo to make room for U Thant's party to fly to Paris, where we took a TWA flight half an hour later for the direct flight to New York. U Thant was in a gloomy mood despite his warm reception in Cairo and Nasser's positive reaction to the moratorium proposal. In New York, Ambassador Rafael of Israel had told Bunche that his government could not accept a moratorium because they believed that 'Nasser wanted war'.

U Thant drafted his second report to the Security Council, and included a paragraph stating that Nasser had accepted his proposals and that Israel had rejected them. In his memoirs,* he said that when he discussed that passage with Ralph Bunche and Alexei Nesterenko, Under Secretary-General (from the Soviet Union), they advised him against its inclusion. They maintained that any mention of this proposal might kill the idea of gaining a breathing spell.

However, the Secretary-General's report to the Security Council mentioned Nasser's plege that the UAR would not be the first to attack. It was in this context that several delegates familiar with the Middle East situation believed U Thant had erred in not following up his visit to Cairo and his high-level talks there with a visit to Israel for talks with its leaders. This might have resulted in Israel's acceptance of his proposals and the securing of a pledge by Israel – similar to that given by the Egyptians – that it would not be the first to attack.

Back in New York, U Thant faced an increasingly hostile press on his decision to withdraw UNEF, and a great deal of precious time, in a crisis situation, was devoted to defending that decision and explaining the reasons behind it.

The Security Council met to consider the Secretary-General's report on the situation. He had indicated that the conflicting positions taken by the UAR and Israel over the Strait of Tiran could lead to war, and warned against the disastrous consequences that would result from such a conflict.

While the Council was in session (May 29, 1967), Nasser gave a press

---

View from the UN – The Memoirs of U Thant (New York: Doubleday, 1978), p. 240.

conference at which he stated that a conflict was inevitable as long as the Palestinian Arabs were not allowed to return to their homes. By contrast, Premier Levi Eshkol of Israel, made a statement over the radio the same evening, saying that Israel would continue to negotiate with the major powers to re-open the Strait of Tiran. Foreign Minister Abba Eban had just returned from a trip to Paris, London and Washington.

On May 30, the Security Council remained deadlocked over the issue of whether the UAR had the legal right to close the Strait of Tiran.

MOMENTUM TOWARDS DISASTER

Britain, the United States and Canada were reported to be considering ways of rallying support for the principle of freedom for all ships in the Gulf. King Hussein of Jordan arrived suddenly in Cairo on May 30, to sign a mutual defence pact with the UAR. Disaster was gaining momentum. Gloom prevailed at the United Nations with the Security Council unable to shoulder its responsibility under the Charter. The United States and the Soviet Union were backing different horses.

In the early hours of June 5, Cairo time, the third Middle East war broke out. Israeli planes struck and destroyed the bulk of the Egyptian Air Force on the ground. Fierce battles raged in Gaza, in Sinai, on the Golan Heights and on the West Bank. In New York, the President of the Security Council, Ambassador Hans Tabor of Denmark, received requests from the representatives of Israel and the UAR for an urgent meeting of the Council. He convened the Council at 9.30 a.m. on June 5. General Rikhye reported that in the course of the fighting there had been Israeli shelling of two UNEF camps, resulting in Indian and Brazilian casualties among members of the UN Force.

On June 6, the UAR government closed the Suez Canal to all shipping and scuttled ships in the waterway, making it impassable. Diplomatic relations with the United States were broken off and US citizens were evacuated from Egypt.

In New York, the Security Council met in the evening and adopted a resolution calling for an immediate cease-fire by all concerned. It was not heeded, and the Council was in continous session to find a way out of that dangerous course. Another cease-fire resolution was adopted. On June 8, Israeli forces reached the Suez Canal, on the Sinai side, after capturing East Jerusalem and occupying the West Bank. It was only then that the UAR accepted the cease-fire. On June 9, Syria announced acceptance of the cease-fire, but accused Israel of continuing its advance. The Council adopted a third resolution demanding that all parties cease hostilities forthwith.

Also on June 9, Reuter carried a bulletin from Cairo that Nasser would hold a press conference later that day and would make an important announcement. When I showed the despatch to U Thant, he said: 'I already know this – he is going to resign but keep this confidential.' I was intrigued and tried to find out the source of this information, but my attempts were unsuccessful. I know he did not learn it from the Egyptians since Ambassador El Kony did not know of it. A few hours later, the news came confirming what U Thant had told me. Nasser, looking haggard and worn out, blamed himself for the military defeat that had befallen his country and announced his resignation. Thousands took to the streets of Cairo, urging him to stay. The National Assembly met late at night and voted unanimously not to accept the President's resignation.

The Security Council met again at 4 a.m. on June 10, at the request of Syria, which accused Israel of advancing on Damascus and bombing it.

U Thant was in constant telex communication with General Bull in Jerusalem. Bull cabled that he had contacted General Dayan in Tel Aviv to make arrangements for a cease-fire and proposed 16.30 hours GMT on June 10 for it to come into effect. Both Syria and Israel accepted.

The same evening, the Soviet Union requested another meeting of the Council to consider Syrian charges that Israel had violated the cease-fire. Ambassador Federenko announced that Moscow had broken off diplomatic relations with Israel. There were verbal clashes between Federenko, on the one hand, and Arthur Goldberg of the United States and Gideon Rafael of Israel on the other. It was a propaganda game of sorts, for while Soviet representatives were making fiery speeches in the Security Council supporting the Arabs and denouncing 'Israeli aggression', Moscow was quietly urging moderation on the Arab capitals.

The Security Council, still deadlocked over the issue of withdrawal of Israeli forces from occupied Arab territories, managed to agree on a resolution calling on both sides to ensure the safety and welfare of peoples under their authority and to respect the 1949 Geneva Convention on the treatment of prisoners of war, and called on Israel to facilitate the return of Arab refugees who had fled the areas occupied by Israeli forces in Jordan, Syria and the Gaza Strip.

The Arab countries, unable to secure a resolution calling on Israel to withdraw, decided to request a Special Emergency Session of the General Assembly. By June 15, the required majority of UN members had indicated their acceptance of this proposal. The Soviet Delegation to the Special Session was headed by Premier Kosygin. He was followed by the Prime Ministers of Bulgaria, Czechoslovakia, Hungary, Poland and Romania.

Also attending were President Al-Atassi of Syria, Foreign Minister Abba Eban of Israel, George Brown of Britain, Maurice Couve de Murville of France, King Hussein of Jordan, and Dr Mahmoud Fawzi of the UAR. It was an array of world leaders that recalled the 1960 Assembly. However, the United States, which had opposed the Special Session, decided to downgrade it. President Johnson stayed in Washington, leaving the task of representing the United States government to Ambassador Goldberg.

The fifth Special Emergency Session of the General Assembly opened on June 17, 1967, with Ambassador Abdel Rahmann Pazwak of Afghanistan presiding. In his speech, Kosygin attacked Israel and introduced a resolution condemning its 'aggression' and demanding that its troops be withdrawn. Replying in the same tone, Abba Eban accused the Soviet Union of feeding an arms race in the Middle East and quoted 'official statements by the Arabs announcing their intention of destroying Israel'. Eban went on to criticise U Thant for agreeing on May 18 to Nasser's request to withdraw UNEF. He demanded: 'What is the use of the fire brigade which vanishes from the scene as soon as the first smoke and flames appear?'

U Thant resented this attack since he had seen Eban a week earlier and explained the reasons that compelled him to take that decision. He decided to reply to Eban when the Assembly reconvened on June 20. In his reply, U Thant stated that UNEF originally had to be stationed only on the UAR side of the line because Israel did not permit the UN force on its side despite the intent of the General Assembly resolution that the United Nations troops should be stationed on both sides. He also recalled his recent discussion with Ambassador Rafael about the possibility of stationing elements of UNEF on the Israeli side and the Ambassador's reply that the idea was unacceptable.

The fifth Special Emergency Session of the General Assembly proceeded without much success in resolving the real issues in the Middle East, and without any progress towards peace. On the positive side, the Assembly adopted, by a large majority, a humanitarian resolution appealing to all governments to assist relief organisations in the Middle East. The second resolution, also adopted by a large majority, was a Pakistani draft declaring 'null and void' the measures taken by Israel to change the status of Jerusalem and calling on Israel to revoke them.

On June 23, while the Assembly was in session, President Johnson and Premier Kosygin met at Glassboro, New Jersey. The information media of course focused their attention on the meeting of the leaders of the two superpowers and all but forgot the General Assembly.

On June 28, Israel announced that Jerusalem was formally 'reunited'. There was a strong reaction in the Assembly. The State Department, in Washington, protested the Israeli action and declared 'that the United States has never recognised such unilateral action by any state in the area as governing the international status of Jerusalem'.

Just before the General Assembly adjourned, on July 5, there was an outbreak of fighting between Israel and the UAR in the Suez Canal area. Both sides requested a meeting of the Security Council. U Thant appealed to the parties to accept the stationing of UN observers on the Canal. After several hours of consultations, Ambassador Makonnen of Ethiopia, the President of the Council, announced a consensus authorising the Secretary-General to proceed with his plan to station observers in the Suez Canal sector.

On July 11, U Thant received a letter from Foreign Minister Eban of Israel, rejecting the General Assembly resolution which requested the annulment of the unilateral unification of Jerusalem. When the Israeli Mission to the UN released the text of the letter, there was an uproar of protest in the United Nations on the eve of the reconvening of the General Assembly.

When it met on July 12, Ambassador Agha Shahi of Pakistan took the floor to revive the Jerusalem issue. Declaring that Israel was attempting to absorb and integrate the Holy City within its territory, he introduced a new draft resolution, reiterating the call on Israel to rescind all measures taken regarding Jerusalem and requesting the Security Council to ensure the implementation of the resolution. The Assembly adopted the Pakistani draft by 100 votes, none against and 18 abstentions. Israel did not participate in the vote, and the United States, in spite of declaring that it did not recognise or accept the measures taken by Israel, abstained because it 'did not believe that peace would be achieved by resolutions dealing with one aspect of the problem'.

During the remaining days of the resumed General Assembly Session, Ambassador Arthur Goldberg of the United States and Foreign Minister Gromyko of the Soviet Union, assisted by Anatoli Dobrynin, the Soviet

Ambassador in Washington, made strenuous efforts to reach agreement on a draft resolution that would link Israeli withdrawal from Arab territories occupied on June 5, with concrete steps towards peace. But these efforts were in vain because their agreed text was unacceptable to the Arabs and was rejected by Israel. The Assembly ended in failure on July 21, 1967.

U Thant appointed Ambassador Ernesto Thalmann, formerly Swiss Observer to the UN, as personal representative of the Secretary-General to Jerusalem. On September 8, Thalmann submitted a report on the situation in Jerusalem which was studied by U Thant and submitted to the General Assembly. The report stated that the Arabs of East Jerusalem were apprehensive about their future and remained opposed to their incorporation into Israel.

On September 24, Israel announced plans for establishing settlements on the West Bank and the Golan Heights. The State Department in Washington declared that settlements conflicted with President Johnson's commitment to support the territorial integrity of all states in the Middle East, and Ambassador Goldberg said in his speech in the General Assembly: 'The cause of peace would not be served if military success blinds a member-state to the fact that its neighbours have rights and interests of their own.'*

In October, while the regular session of the General Assembly was in session, Vasily Kuznetsov, first Soviet Deputy Foreign Minister, arrived in New York to take charge of the Soviet Delegation. In his talks with U Thant, he indicated that Moscow favoured a return to the Security Council. Goldberg, who had a long discussion with Foreign Minister Riad of the UAR, reported to U Thant that Cairo was ready to accept the idea of a special representative of the Secretary-General for the Middle East.

The British Representative to the United Nations was Lord Caradon (formerly Sir Hugh Foot), an old Middle East hand, highly respected by Arabs and Israelis alike. Together with his aides, and with the active collaboration of Goldberg, Caradon put together the elements for a draft resolution dealing with the substance of the problem. It was unanimously adopted by the Security Council on November 22, 1967. On that day, Caradon was nicknamed 'the father of 242', referring to the famous resolution no. 242, a breakthrough that had the support of the big powers and was acceptable to the UAR as well as Israel. The resolution reads:

'Emphasising the inadmissibility of the acquisition of territory by war and

*UN Assembly Records, Oct. 30, 1967.

the need to work for a just and lasting peace in which every state in the area can live in security

'Emphasising further that all Member States in their acceptance of the Charter of the United Nations have undertaken a commitment to act in accordance with article 2 of the Charter

'1. Affirms that the fulfilment of Charter principles requires the establishment of a just and lasting peace in the Middle East which should include the application of both the following principles:

'(i) Withdrawal of Israeli armed forces from territories occupied in the recent conflict;

'(ii) Termination of all claims or states of belligerency and respect for and acknowledgement of the sovereignty, territorial integrity and political independence of every State in the area and their right to live in peace within secure and recognised boundaries free from threat or acts of force;

'2. Affirms further the necessity

'(a) For guaranteeing freedom of navigation through international waterways in the area;

'(b) For achieving a just settlement of the refugee problem;

'(c) For guaranteeing the territorial inviolability and political independence of every State in the area, through measures including the establishment of demilitarised zones;

'3. Requests the Secretary-General to designate a Special Representative to proceed to the Middle East to establish and maintain contacts with the States concerned in order to promote agreement and ,assist efforts to achieve a peaceful and acceptable settlement in accordance with the provisions and principles in this resolution.

'4. Requests the Secretary-General to report to the Security Council on the progress of the efforts of the Special Representative as soon as possible.'

U Thant appointed Gunnar Jarring, Swedish Ambassador to Moscow and a former permanent representative of his country to the UN, as Special Representative to the Middle East. Jarring embarked on his difficult task with the dedication of a veteran diplomat undertaking an impossible mission. He made several trips to the area and conferred with the leaders of both sides. Meanwhile, the spiral of violence, attacks and counter-attacks between the Arabs and Israel continued unabated.

Nasser died on September 28, 1970, and was succeeded by Vice President Anwar Sadat. Diplomatic efforts for a peaceful settlement in the Middle East continued in 1971 and 1972 without progress. The Jarring mission fell into abeyance since it never received the full support of the Big Four (Britain, France, the United States and the Soviet Union).

The October war broke out in 1973. After heavy fighting on the Egyptian and Syrian fronts, a cease-fire was effected as a result of strong Soviet and American pressures. Henry Kissinger, President Nixon's Secretary of State, innovated his shuttle diplomacy between Israel and Egypt, and later between Israel and Syria, and succeeded in achieving disengagement agreements between the warring parties. A relatively quiet period followed, but peace eluded all efforts.

In November 1977, President Anwar Sadat of Egypt made his 'sacred mission' to Israel, thus opening a new page in the history of the Middle East. I was in Geneva on the evening of November 19 when Swiss TV carried, live, Sadat's arrival in Jerusalem and his speech to the Knesset on November 20. I sat watching and listening to every word, wondering whether it was all a dream – and I wept.

The peace process he initiated bore fruit at Camp David, a year later in 1978. With the active participation of President Jimmy Carter of the United States, President Sadat of Egypt and Premier Begin of Israel concluded their 'framework for peace', and the peace treaty between Egypt and Israel was signed.

Henry Kissinger, who met Anwar Sadat in 1973 and established a friendship and rapport with him in the years that followed, wrote the most beautiful appreciation of Sadat after his savage assasination in Cairo on October 6, 1981: 'In his own way, Sadat has moved towards the age-old Egyptian dream of immortality. Peace will be his pyramid. It has been an honour to be one of his contemporaries.'[*]

PEACE VINDICATED

The savage, senseless Iraq-Iran war, which started in September 1980, was still raging in 1988. In its shadow, an urgent Arab Summit (15th) met in Amman in November 1987. King Hussein of Jordan took the initiative in convening the Summit to adopt a common stand against Iran's Islamic revolution that was threatening to engulf every Arab regime. Immediately following the Summit nine Arab countries, including Saudi Arabia, Morocco and Iraq, renewed full diplomatic

[*]*Time* magazine, October 19, 1981.

relations with Egypt – relations they had severed in protest at the Peace Treaty between Egypt and Israel signed in 1979.

For ten years, Arab leaders had pursued a policy of 'no war – no peace' towards Israel – a policy that did little to alleviate the sufferings of Palestinians living under Israeli occupation in Gaza and on the West Bank. The Amman Summit unanimously endorsed a call for an international peace conference, under UN auspices, to seek a just solution of the Palestine problem. All hopes were pinned on such a conference.

Ironically, the very idea of an international conference was first proposed by President Sadat in a speech before Egypt's National Assembly in Cairo on October 16, 1973.* Subsequently, the Geneva Conference – with the participation of the United States and the Soviet Union – had taken place in December 1973, but it had adjourned without any substantive results.

*Article by Dr Boutros B. Ghali, Egypt's Minister of State for Foreign Affairs, commemorating the tenth anniversary of Sadat's historic visit to Jerusalem (*Al Ahram*, Nov. 19, 1987).

UNITED NATIONS NATIONS UNIES

NEW YORK

CABLE ADDRESS · UNATIONS NEWYORK · ADRESSE TELEGRAPHIQUE

FERENCE: # SG also told the President that on his way to Cairo, he got information at Paris airport regarding the closing of the Gulf of Aquaba. To be frank he was very much surprised, since in his view was was inevitable, for that action.

‡ Regarding the closing of the Gulf of Aquaba, President said that the decision had been made some time earlier. The question was the timing of the ~~decision~~ announcement of the decision. If the announcement ~~were to be made~~ made after SG's visit to Cairo, it would be widely interpreted that SG had been snubbed, so it was decided to announce it before SG's arrival.

Handwritten note by U Thant mentioning his warning to President Nasser of the consequences of closing the Straits of Tiran. There follows a summary record, with his annotations, of his talks with the President.

Secret

MEETING WITH PRESIDENT NASSER
Cairo - 24 May 1967

Meeting attended by:

Secretary-General   Mr. Mahmoud Fawzy, Deputy President
Major-General I. J. Rikhye   for Foreign Affairs
                                     Mr. Mahmoud Riad, Foreign Minister

1. The President received the SG at his residence at 2000 hours on [for dinner and discussion] 24 May 1967. The SG opened the conversation by saying that he was required to make a report to the Security Council on his visit to Cairo. He would therefore like to have the President's reaction to his proposal on declaring a moratorium in the Gulf of Aqaba. #

2. The President briefly stated the position of the UAR along the same lines as the Foreign Minister during SG's meeting with him earlier in the day. President said that already two ships entering the Gulf had been searched by the UAR; however, he wished to help the UN in restoring peace, especially when it was threatened by the attitude of Israel who had given every indication of invading Sharm el Sheikh. UAR forces were prepared to defend themselves. President would, however, accept SG's proposal for a moratorium for a period of

two weeks. It was no longer possible for him to physically withdraw his blockade but he would issue orders that his people in the Gulf would be "good boys" as long as Israel on its part complied with SG's request.

3. SG stated that he would cable Bunche tonight ~~to carry out consul~~ tations to persuade Israel not to send shipping through the Gulf ~~and other countries~~ to refrain from sending strategic materials to Eilat as defined by the UAR.

- 2 -

4. The question of UN supervising compliance of this agreement during the two-week moratorium period was considered and rejected by the President on the grounds of breach of armed forces' security involved with any UN presence.

5. The President said that UAR had achieved its goal by returning to pre-1956 position, with one difference: that they were now in a . position to defend their country and their rights. He had accepted offer of troops from Algeria, Kuwait, and Iraq. UAR did not require military assistance from any other Arab country, but it was important

to agree to token contributions in the interest of the morale of the
Arab world. The populace of these countries had received a great
fillip in their morale, and many volunteers were offering themselves
for the fight against Israel.

6. President covered the position of the major Powers and blocs on
the question of the Gulf blockade. He said that the US had always
supported Israel. The Russians have declared their support for the
UAR. France was neutral, and the UK followed the US line. The line-
up was typical of the present division amongst the major Powers. UAR
relations with US have deteriorated over the years because of a clash
of mutual interests. US had applied economic pressure and stopped
assistance last year. UAR had to reduce its industrial production and
to limit importation of raw material to provide sufficient hard
currency to buy food. The position had improved for this year. The
President had declined, however, any offers of assistance from US,
UK, and West Germany. His position also was that if credits were made
available, interest on past loans would be paid. He had therefore
refused to pay interest on loans to US, UK, and West Germany. The

International

- 3 -

World/Monetary Fund had also applied some pressures as had the
International Bank. But his position was, if no more credits, no
payment of past dues and interest. France and Italy had renegotiated
medium loans to long-term loans. They had also been able to obtain
some credit elsewhere, and the UAR economic position had somewhat
improved. He concluded by stating UAR's determination to retain its
independence of action and to defend its sovereignty and its rights.

7. The SG asked President's comments on the possibility of appointment of a special representative to the area with possible location
at Gaza. The President said that US and Canada had in 1957 attempted
to place Gaza Strip under UNEF administration. This was unacceptable
to UAR then as it would be any appointment which might indicate
international presence after withdrawal of UNEF by anyone other than
EIMAC. The President offered, however, to accept any UN diplomatic
presence in Cairo and assured the SG of his fullest co-operation.

8. During a discussion on possible developments during the Security
Council meeting, FM said that the item inscribed was the Middle East.
There were lots of trouble spots in the Middle East besides the Gulf

of Aqaba, and it would appear that a free-for-all discussion would take place in the Security Council. The SG said that the Security Council was involved in a procedural wrangle and would probably waste time on it. The President said that he had already instructed the FM to open the UN files on the failure on the part of Israel to comply with UN resolutions. On the other hand, Egypt had always supported and co-operated with the UN and would continue to do so.

9. The President then raised the question of removal and disposal of UNEF property. He said that their armed forces would be prepared to buy any items for disposal.

- 4 -

10. Rikhye informed President of the arrangements already made that certain items, including vehicles, radio sets, and other military type equipment, would be transferred to Pisa and Jerusalem as required. Other items for disposal were being sorted out, and the UAR would be informed about availability.

11. The SG confirmed arrangements, especially about the transfer of

certain items to Pisa and Jerusalem. The President expressed his acceptance of such an arrangement and promised his fullest co-operation. He said that if any difficulties arose, these should be brought to the notice of the armed forces authorities who had his instructions to co-operate with UN.

12. The President then offered to the SG the highest UAR military decoration for UNEF. At first this was misunderstood; SG and Rikhye thought the offer was for individual officers and men. The President, however, clarified the point by saying that he was offering a decoration for UNEF as a whole along the customary military lines when a whole unit or a formation is decorated. The SG said that he would like to give further consideration to this generous offer of the President and would send him a reply from New York.

13. The President stated his gratitude to UNEF and to UN for helping the UAR in 1956 and since then till now. He conveyed his great appreciation for the assistance rendered by UNEF in keeping and maintaining peace in the area. He asked Rikhye to convey his personal thanks to all ranks for the services rendered to the UAR and for keeping peace in the area.

7

EPISODES

WEST IRIAN

From the beginning of his administration, U Thant demonstrated that he would be an activist in the sense that he would use his office as an instrument for settling disputes – often without waiting for a directive from the Security Council or from the General Assembly. His first intervention of this kind came on December 14, 1961, when he sent messages to the Governments of India and Portugal appealing to them to use restraint in their dispute over the Portuguese territories of Goa, Daman and Diu – small enclaves situated along the west coast of India. The appeal was not heeded and Indian troops seized the territories four days later.

On December 19, 1961, U Thant appealed to the Netherlands and Indonesia to seek a peaceful solution to their dispute over West Irian (West New Guinea). He sent identical cables to Jan de Quay, Prime Minister of the Netherlands, and Achmed Sukarno, President of Indonesia, urging both to refrain from any action that would give rise to a threat to peace and security.

On January 15, 1962, he sent two additional cables to the two leaders expressing his deep concern over a clash between Dutch and Indonesian naval vessels in connection with the dispute. This was followed by two more cables, on January 17, asking the two leaders to instruct their Permanent Representatives to discuss with the Secretary-General the possibilities for a peaceful settlement of the question in conformity with the purposes and principles of the United Nations Charter.

These appeals constituted the first of several measures culminating in a settlement of the problem through U Thant's own mediation and that of his personal representative, Ambassador Ellsworth Bunker from the United States. Under U Thant's direction and with the approval of the General Assembly, the United Nations actually administered the territory of West Irian during a brief transitional period between the withdrawal of the Netherlands authorities and the take-over by the Indonesians.

This was the first time that such an operation had ever been undertaken by the United Nations. It was also the first time the parties to a dispute had paid the total costs of a United Nations intervention.

On August 15, 1962, at a ceremony, appropriately held in the Security Council Chamber, Indonesia and the Netherlands signed an agreement on the future of the previously disputed territory. In his statement at the ceremony, U Thant congratulated the two governments on their willingness to settle the question by peaceful negotiations, and expressed his gratitude to Ambassador Bunker who had acted on his behalf during the preliminary negotiations between the two governments and whose diplomatic skill had contributed to the agreement.

On September 2, 1962, the General Assembly adopted a resolution sponsored by Indonesia and the Netherlands which brought the agreement into force.

The agreement called for a phased transfer of the West Irian territory from the Netherlands to Indonesia with the United Nations taking over administration of the territory for the first stage and an eventual plebiscite before 1969 to permit the people to decide their own future. The transfer of administration of West Irian to Indonesia took place on May 1, 1963. It was hailed as an important success for both U Thant and the United Nations. However, once Indonesia took over the administration of the territory it decided not to conduct a supervised plebiscite as pledged.

While U Thant's diplomacy in 1962 undoubtedly served to defuse a dangerous international situation, retrospectively it may seem that Indonesia took advantage of the worldwide move towards decolonisation to annex and in effect re-colonise a territory which, because all its indigenous inhabitants were Papuans and not Indonesians, should instead have become completely independent a few years later, following a longer period of preparation. The Indonesians' refusal of a plebiscite and flooding of the territory with settlers from overcrowded Java makes the transfer of sovereignty that took place in the early 1960s seem a tragic mistake.

WINDING UP THE CONGO OPERATION

The United Nations Operation in the Congo (ONUC according to its French initials) was established by the Security Council on the initiative of Secretary-General Dag Hammarskjöld. After he lost his life in the search for peace in the Congo, U Thant inherited the problem and was forced to deal with its complexities from the first day after his appointment as Acting Secretary-General on November 3, 1961.

On November 13, the Security Council met at the request of three African countries (Ethiopia, Nigeria, Sudan) and adopted on November 24 a resolution deploring secessionist acts in Katanga, and authorised the Secretary-General to use force to remove all foreign mercenaries from the Congo.

But Tshombe, who had proclaimed his independence in Katanga, continued to defy ONUC. His gendarmerie installed roadblocks to hamper the movement of the UN forces, and there were skirmishes. Reports from ONUC headquarters to the United Nations in New York indicated a deliberate plan to isolate the UN troops in Elisabethville, the capital of Katanga.

Hostilities between the UN forces and Tshombe's gendarmerie started on December 2, 1961. ONUC moved to seize positions that would safeguard their freedom of movement. By December 19, UN forces had reached their objectives and the fighting stopped. Tshombe left Elisabethville for talks with Cyrille Adoula, the Prime Minister of the central government at the UN base at Kitona. The United States played a major role in arranging the meeting and persuading Tshombe to participate. An agreement was signed in which Tshombe pledged to accept the authority of Leopoldville and to respect UN resolutions.

On February 25, 1962, the Provincial Assembly of Katanga met and accepted the Kitona declaration. Premier Adoula invited Tshombe to Leopoldville. He arrived in March, and the discussions concentrated on putting an end to the secession of Katanga. But the honeymoon between Adoula and the United Nations, on the one hand, and Tshombe, on the other, did not last. No sooner had Tshombe returned to Elisabethville than he started to agitate against the UN forces stationed in Katanga. Meanwhile, U Thant had appointed Robert Gardiner, of Ghana, as UN representative in the Congo, the top civilian post in charge of ONUC. (Rajeshwar Dayal had been relieved of his duties as UN Representative in the Congo at his own request, on May 25, 1961, by Hammarskjöld, who appointed Mekki Abbas, from the Sudan, as acting representative. Abbas in turn resigned and Sture Linner, a Swede, succeeded him as officer-in-charge on September 1, 1961, a little over two weeks before Hammarskjöld's death.)

It was in this context that while on an official visit to Finland, U Thant described Tshombe and his aides at a press conference in Helsinki on July 20, 1961, as 'a bunch of clowns'. It was a most undiplomatic phrase, coming from the Secretary-General of the UN! But, despite U Thant's proverbial mildness, one could not be surprised because

Tshombe was a constant headache to the United Nations. He made promises which he did not keep, and his mercenaries would disappear only to re-surface again harrassing the UN force. U Thant was fed up with him, and, caught in an unguarded moment, he spoke his mind.

A plan for national conciliation, referred to as 'U Thant's plan', was presented to Leopoldville and Elisabethville in August 1962. It contained the drafting of a federal constitution, formation of a central government representing all the country's provinces, a unified currency, integration of all military units in one national army, the sharing of revenues between Leopoldville and the provincial governments, and the proclamation of a general amnesty. Adoula accepted it right away, and Tshombe wrote that he favoured it. But three weeks later he had reservations, mostly regarding the clauses relating to revenues, since Katanga was by far the Congo's richest province in mineral resources.

In December 1962, the gendarmerie harrassed and fired upon United Nations forces in Katanga. They shot down a UN helicopter, killing an Indian officer serving with ONUC. Responding to an urgent request from Robert Gardiner and General Prem Chand, the Indian Commander of UN forces, U Thant reluctantly issued the order to remove the gendarmerie and the mercenaries from Elisabethville. The British and Belgian governments voiced serious objections and urged him to rescind the order. They protested that any military action by the United Nations would result in the destruction of the Union Minière, the vast Belgian-owned industrial complex in Katanga. U Thant cabled Gardiner, informing him of the warning delivered by the two governments and asking for his comments.

That was on December 30. Somehow, there was a breakdown in communications between Leopoldville and UN Headquarters in New York. On January 3, 1963, Gardiner cabled that UN forces (consisting of units from India, Ethiopia, Tunisia, Ireland, Sweden and Ghana, boosted by ten fighter planes and two reconaissance aircraft provided by Ethiopia) had entered the town of Jadotville, an important junction. They had met no opposition and the mercenaries had fled. They moved forward, destroying two air bases and occupying more vantage points in Katanga.

On January 14, 1963, the Belgian government transmitted to U Thant a message from Tshombe declaring his willingness to put an end to secession, and allow UN troops complete freedom of movement, and demanding the granting of amnesty by the central government to all members of his government. President Kasavubu of the Congo confirmed to U Thant that the amnesty proclamation was still valid. Meanwhile UN forces fanned out, and succeeded in restoring law and order throughout Katanga.

On October 18, 1963, the UN General Assembly, at the request of the government of the Congo, voted to continue the UN operation till June 30, 1964. On June 29, U Thant submitted a comprehensive report to the Security Council on the withdrawal of the UN forces from the Congo. It stated: 'The province of Katanga slowly returned to normal. The integration of the gendarmerie into the national army proceeded in a satisfactory fashion. ONUC assisted the Congolese authorities in instituting security measures throughout Katanga and carried out joint patrols. In Leopoldville, the situation remained satisfactory. ONUC maintained close liaison with the Congolese military and police.

'The Government of the Congo had announced, in October 1963 and in April 1964, that it had foiled plots against the regime. Tribal and political disorders took place in the Kwilu province, Kisandgi and other areas. Religious missions were attacked. ONUC, in cooperation with local authorities, launched rescue operations to save missionaries, nuns and personnel of UN Agencies, working on technical assistance in far out districts and brought them to safety in Leopoldville.'

In conclusion, the report made the following points: 'The total cost of the military and civilian operations up to June 30, 1964, came to $433 million US dollars. This figure included voluntary donations for famine relief as well as contributions, in local currency, from the Congolese Government. The withdrawal of the United Nations Force from the Congo, completed on June 30, 1964, marked the end of only the military phase of the massive assistance operations which the UN conducted in the Congo. Civilian operations, technical assistance and special fund activities continued subject to the extent that financial and other resources were available and the wishes of the Government of the Congo.'*

The military operation ended almost exactly four years after the Security Council had authorised UN intervention to prevent the secession of Katanga. The United Nations objectives had, in a large measure, been fulfilled. These included the preservation of the territorial integrity of the Congo, the elimination of foreign military personnel and mercenaries, and the prevention of a civil war. The question of maintaining law and order was the responsibility of the Congolese government.

*Security Council Official Records document S/5784 (June 1964).

Although disorders continued, the withdrawal had been carried out with the full consent of the Congolese authorities.

With a strength of more than 20,000 UN troops at its peak, ONUC was by far the largest peacekeeping operation ever launched by the United Nations. Its casualties totalled 235.

Shortly after the withdrawal of the United Nations Force, on July 9, 1964, Adoula resigned and President Kasavubu appointed Tshombe Prime Minister. Rebels established a rival government in Stanleyville and seized 1,000 foreign nationals as hostages. Tshombe appealed to Belgium for military assistance. Belgian commandos were dispatched and flown in by United States military aircraft. They carried out a rescue operation and freed the hostages.

The Security Council met on December 1, 1964, to consider the deteriorating situation in the Congo at the request of African states as well as the government of the Congo.

Belgium vehemently defended its military intervention, at the request of the Congolese government, to save innocent civilians from certain death. The United States, Britain and Italy defended the Belgian action, while the Soviet Union assailed it. An acrimonious debate with unfortunate racial overtones ensued. On December 30, the Security Council adopted a compromise resolution urging all states not to intervene in the domestic affairs of the Congo.

Tshombe's tenure of office, as Prime Minister of the Congo, was beset by difficulties, domestic as well as foreign. There was the rebellion in Stanleyville. The Organisation of African Unity (OAU) was hostile, and declined to invite him to the African Summit scheduled for July 1964 in Cairo. Tshombe retaliated by declaring that he would boycott the meeting. Inside the Congo, reports by the opposition claimed that Tshombe was the instigator in the murder of Lumumba. The Congolese Parliament met and deprived him of membership.

In October 1965, Tshombe opted to leave the country. Flying in his private plane, he took members of his family and a small entourage to political asylum in Spain. He lived in seclusion, near Madrid. On July 1, 1967, Tshombe's name was in the news again. On June 30, his plane, while flying from Ibiza to Majorca was hijacked by a French mercenary (F. Bodeman) who forced it to land in Algiers. The Algerians put Tshombe and his party under house-arrest, in a villa in the suburbs, and refused to allow them to go back to Spain. In the Congo, Colonel Mobutu came to power after a military coup. Twice, he asked the Algerian Government to extradite Tshombe. In a peculiar way, the

Algerians, while regarding Tshombe as a traitor, were anxious to demonstrate their independence and refused Mobutu's request.

Up till today the full story behind Algeria's attitude and the hijacking has not been revealed in spite of a series of newspaper accounts and interpretations as recently as 1982. On June 30, 1969, Tshombe, a virtual prisoner, died of a heart attack in his villa near Algiers.

INDIA–PAKISTAN

In August 1965 hostilities broke out between India and Pakistan over Kashmir, and the cease-fire agreement of July 29, 1949 collapsed. (The dispute over Kashmir had been before the UN since 1948, India maintaining that the province was part of India and Pakistan insisting that the people of Kashmir should be allowed to exercise the right of self-determination. The UN Security Council had placed a UN military observer group, UNMOGIP, there under the command of General R.H. Nimmo of Australia).

When the situation deteriorated further, U Thant despatched, on September 1, two identical appeals to Prime Minister Lal Bahadur Shastri of India and to President Ayub Khan of Pakistan requesting that their military forces pull back to the 1949 cease-fire line. The same day, Ambassador Arthur Goldberg of the United States, who was President of the Security Council for that month, endorsed U Thant's appeal and initiated a series of informal meetings with members of the Council and the Secretary-General to discuss the situation.

On September 4, Goldberg called a meeting of the Security Council. A resolution urging a cease-fire, and requesting both sides to cooperate with the UN observer group, was adopted. This was not heeded, and the fighting continued. The Security Council met once more, on September 6. Again, it called on India and Pakistan to stop the hostilities immediately and requested the Secretary-General 'to exert every possible effort towards that end'. U Thant immediately accepted that responsibility and discussed with Goldberg, as President of the Council, the modalities of his mission to the sub-continent. Since all flights between India and Pakistan were cancelled on account of the war, Ambassador Goldberg offered a United States plane to fly U Thant and his party from Teheran. The party consisted of Brian Urquhart (later UN Under Secretary-General for Special Political Affairs); myself, as press officer for the Secretary-General; Donald Thomas, security guard and personal aide; and Lucien Lemieux, private secretary.

We left New York on a BOAC flight on the evening of September 7. In London, where we had a brief stopover, a small group of militant Pakistani students had gathered outside the airport hotel. As the students saw U Thant getting out of his car, to enter the hotel, they shouted: 'Down with U Thant! Down with the United Nations!' We were shaken by this hostile reception and two policemen chased the demonstrators away.

The plane arrived in Teheran after midnight. Despite the late hour, Prime Minister Hoveda (executed by Khomeini's regime after the Iranian revolution) was at the airport to greet the Secretary-General. He ordered the Shah's luxurious airport lounge to be opened and put it at U Thant's disposal. After a rest and a light supper, we boarded the United States plane which flew us to Karachi, landing there the next morning.

A large number of correspondents were waiting. U Thant answered their questions without elaborating on the substance, and managed to extricate himself after a few minutes. The reporters did not press him further and were content with what he had said.

From Karachi, we travelled by air to Rawalpindi where he was met by Zulfiqar Ali Bhutto, the Foreign Minister of Pakistan, and his senior aides. After a brief discussion, U Thant proceeded to the President's residence, where he had a long meeting with President Ayub Khan. In the talks, U Thant stressed that his mandate from the Security Council was to achieve an immediate cease-fire while the President maintained that the Council should also concern itself with the Kashmir problem. There was no agreement.

On September 10, U Thant visited the UN observers' offices in Rawalpindi and again met Bhutto. With U Thant emphasising the threat to world peace and Bhutto insisting on the rights of the people of Kashmir, this meeting was also unproductive. On a personal note, U Thant mentioned that one of his dreams was to visit Taxila, once the seat of the oldest Buddhist university in the world. After lunch, Bhutto graciously took him in his car to the ruined city, about an hour's drive from Rawalpindi.

U Thant had a second inconclusive meeting with President Ayub Khan before leaving Pakistan, on September 11, by the same US plane that had flown us from Teheran. We landed in New Delhi on September 12 after a roundabout flight with a stop at Bombay.

The Indian government put us up at the President's palace (Rashtrapati Bhavan), one of the most beautiful palaces I had ever seen. Its splendour reminded me of King Farouk's fabled palaces in Egypt. The suite assigned to me was larger than my whole apartment in Manhattan. After a courtesy call on President Radhakrishnan of India, U Thant called on Prime Minister Shastri at his private residence, a small and modest house in the Delhi suburbs. U Thant informed him of his intention to address identical appeals to India and Pakistan for a cease-fire and withdrawal of troops. With the help of Brian Urquhart, the appeals were drafted later in the day and delivered to Rawalpindi and New Delhi at the same time that evening. They were not heeded, as each party imposed conditions for accepting the cease-fire.

The following day, a second appeal was sent. This was accepted by Prime Minister Shastri without conditions, but President Ayub Khan insisted on a cease-fire coupled with a political settlement of the Kashmir problem. A third and final appeal was despatched on September 15, minutes before U Thant's departure, from New Delhi, for Bombay *en route* to New York.

The Air India plane landed at Kennedy airport early in the afternoon of September 16. To greet U Thant, Ambassador Goldberg, President of the Security Council, had assembled all members of the Council at the airport. It was a magnificent gesture of support which left U Thant speechless with gratitude. Back at his office, the same day, he submitted a report to the Security Council outlining his talks with the leaders of India and Pakistan. He dwelt at length on how in the course of the conflict their respective positions had hardened. The report stated that, although there was a general willingness to put an end to the hostilities, an effective cease-fire had not materialised. The Security Council met on September 17 and 18, but because there was no agreement on a draft resolution acceptable to the two parties, it was deadlocked.

At a third meeting in the early hours of September 19, the Council adopted a resolution calling for a cease-fire to become effective on September 22, and withdrawal of all military forces to positions held before August 5 when the hostilities had begun. The resolution also stated that the Council would consider what steps could be taken to help settle the political problem. India agreed to comply, while Pakistan informed U Thant that Foreign Minister Bhutto was on his way to New York with an urgent message from his President. The Security Council convened in the early morning of September 21, to hear an eloquent and dramatic speech from Bhutto about the just rights of the people of Kashmir. He finally declared that Pakistan troops had been ordered to cease-fire.

But sporadic fighting continued, and on October 22, Pakistan asked for an urgent meeting of the Council, alleging that India was planning a new offensive. The Council met again on November 5 and passed a resolution calling for the withdrawal of troops and requesting represen- tatives from India and Pakistan to meet a representative of the Secretary- General to discuss the modalities of withdrawal. U Thant appointed General Tulio Marambio of Chile as representative of the Secretary- General for that purpose.

Meanwhile, there was an unexpected development. The Soviet Union, concerned over the continuing fighting between India and Pakistan and alarmed over the covert support China was offering Pakistan, decided to move and outmanoeuvre Peking. Prime Minister Alexei Kosygin invited Premier Shastri of India and President Khan of Pakistan to a meeting with him in Tashkent. The invitation was issued on December 8, 1965, and the meeting took place on January 4, 1966. Six days of intensive diplomatic mediation by Kosygin produced the Tashkent Declaration, signed by Shastri and Khan on January 10, 1966. In the declaration, the two leaders pledged to restore peaceful relations between their two countries and undertook to settle their differences through peaceful means. They agreed on the withdrawal of troops and the repatriation of prisoners of war.

U Thant paid a warm tribute to Prime Minister Kosygin's skill in negotiating the declaration, and Ralph Bunche, who worked closely with U Thant on the India–Pakistan conflict, and who was not known for his pro-Soviet sentiments, said to Ambassador Federenko of the Soviet Union outside the Security Council Chamber: 'I do not know how he did it – I take my hat off to Prime Minister Kosygin.' Federenko smiled and said 'Thank You.'

Fate, or perhaps an act of God, helped cement the declaration and soothe the hatred between Indians and Pakistanis. Two hours after the signing ceremony of the declaration, at Tashkent, Prime Minister Shastri died suddenly of a heart attack. It was a moving picture that I saw on American television: the tall imposing figures of President Ayub Khan of Pakistan and Premier Kosygin, among the pall-bearers, carrying the body of Shastri, draped in white, to a waiting Indian plane to carry him for burial in his homeland.

THE INVASION OF CZECHOSLOVAKIA

It was one a.m. on August 21, 1968, when the telephone rang in my apartment in Manhattan. The caller was William Oatis of the Associated

Press, who gave me the news that Soviet troops together with forces of other Warsaw Pact members had invaded Czechoslovakia.

For several days, the information media had been publishing news about the strained relations between the government of Alexander Dubček in Prague, and the Kremlin. *Pravda* and *Izvestia* were complaining bitterly of the behaviour of the Czechoslovak press and radio and their criticism of the Soviet Union. A strong Soviet reaction was not unexpected, but no one predicted an invasion.

Now that the invasion had taken place, Oatis wanted to know U Thant's reaction, as Secretary-General, and whether the Security Council would meet. I said that in spite of the hour, I must speak to the SG first, and receive his instructions on what to say on such a serious problem. I cautioned Oatis that I doubted whether U Thant would authorise an off-the-cuff comment.

I put down the receiver and before I had time to call the duty officer at the UN building, identify myself and ask him to connect me on the 'tieline' with the Secretary-General at his residence, the telephone rang again. This time, it was Bruce Munn of UPI with the same news and questions. I replied in the same vein as before.

I rang up the UN and was put through. U Thant must have been sitting by the telephone for he answered immediately. He had heard the news on the radio, but did not want to make a comment right away. However, I was not to say 'No comment', he continued, for that in itself, might be misconstrued. He also told me that he wanted to consult with Ambassador José Castro of Brazil, who was President of the Security Council for the month of August. In saying that, he was thinking out loud without authorising what should be said to the press at the moment. At the end of the conversation, he asked me to stall as much as possible and call him back.

I finished my conversation with him and put down the telephone only to hear it ring again. This time it was Reuters, followed by the *New York Times*. I said I was waiting for instructions and hoped to have something later in the day. On the question of the Security Council, I said I had no guidance.

I called back U Thant to ask what to say. As always, in matters relating to the press, he was keen to know who had called – for he knew every correspondent at UN Headquarters – and what I had said. The fact that our conversation was taking place about 2.00 a.m. did not change anything in this regard. Finally, he authorised me to say that the Secretary-General would issue a formal statement on the invasion.

When I enquired about the Security Council, he answered that no request had been made for a meeting, probably because members of the Council were asleep at that hour and were not glued to their radios. But he thought the Council would meet. U Thant finished the conversation by urging me to be extra careful in everything I said.

Bruce Munn called again and I informed him that a statement by the Secretary-General would be issued at noon. Again, he asked about the Security Council. Whether it was the time element or just a slip of the tongue, I said a meeting was expected but so far no requests had been received. He hung up and called his office to phone a bulletin 'The Security Council will meet today to take up the Soviet invasion of Czechoslovakia, UPI has learned from United Nations sources.' Fortunately, he did not quote me by name, and his bulletin was too late to make the morning papers.

It was impossible to go back to sleep. I went to my office at the United Nations at 9.00 a.m., to be told by the duty officer that the Secretary-General had just come in. I went straight to his office. His first remark was that he hoped I managed to go back to sleep; he had not been able to do so. He asked if I had seen the latest edition of the *New York Times* where I was quoted by name on its front page, saying that U Thant would issue a statement on the Soviet invasion of Czechoslovakia.

He informed me that he had asked Ambassador Jacob Malik of the Soviet Union and G. Muzik, the Chargé d'Affaires of Czechoslovakia, to come and see him separately. He subsequently entered his office asking not to be disturbed. Half an hour later he summoned C.V. Narasimhan, his *Chef de Cabinet*, and they went over the draft of his statement which was completed and typed before Ambassador Malik's arrival.

Malik came at 10.30 and gave U Thant a copy of the Soviet Government's statement on the 'intervention' in Czechoslovakia 'at the request of its leaders'. In response U Thant stated that the invasion was a violation of the UN Charter and a serious blow to détente, and gave him a copy of the statement he was issuing to the press at noon. Malik read it carefully, put it in his pocket and left without comment. On his way out, he refused to talk to the press.

An hour later, Muzik came. He informed U Thant that Czechoslovakia's Foreign Minister Jiři Hajek, who was taking a vacation in Yugoslavia, was unable to return to Prague because all communications and transportation had been cut off. U Thant informed him that he had decided to cancel his trip to Prague as well as Vienna and Geneva, which had been planned for some time. On a personal note, he expressed his deep regret. He had been looking forward to visiting Prague again and receiving an honorary degree from Charles University, one of the oldest universities in Europe (in fact, U Thant had been scheduled to leave New York the following day, August 22). After his meeting with Muzik he called Bill Powell and me into his office. He gave us a copy of his statement to be read at the noon briefing. I went over it carefully and discussed what should be said in case of subsequent questions.

Room 226, our regular press briefing room, was packed with correspondents. There was a United Nations TV camera, acting as a pool for the TV networks. Powell said 'Maybe I should read it' – I reminded him of our agreement that he should handle questions relating to the Middle East while I dealt with questions on Vietnam and topics involving the United States or the Soviet Union. It was an understanding that we had reached during the Middle East crisis to avoid personal embarrassment to either of us. It would not have been appropriate for Powell as an American to read a statement denouncing or criticising the United States or, for that matter, the Soviet Union. By the same token it was uncomfortable for an Egyptian to make remarks against either Israel or Egypt. When we presented this formulation to U Thant he gave us his blessing and asked us to stick to it.

I started reading the statement on behalf of the Secretary-General – slowly, at the request of the electronic media: 'This morning, the Secretary-General has had meetings with the heads of missions directly concerned with the events in Czechoslovakia and with the President of the Security Council.

'The Secretary-General does not yet have full official information in regard to the most recent developments and the circumstances which led to them. It is well known, however, that the Secretary-General deplores any resort to force to settle international problems, wherever they may occur, in contravention of the Charter of the United Nations.

'In the present case, the Secretary-General regards the developments in Czechoslovakia as yet another serious blow to the concepts of international order and morality which form the basis of the Charter of the United Nations and for which the United Nations has been striving all these years. It is also a grave setback to the East-West détente which seemed to be re-emerging in recent months, and to which the Secretary-General attaches the greatest importance. He had appealed to the government of the Union of Soviet Socialist Republics to exercise the utmost restraint in its relations with the government and people of

Czechoslovakia, and strongly hopes that this appeal will be heeded by the government of the Union of Soviet Socialist Republics and its Warsaw Pact allies.

'In the circumstances, the Secretary-General has cancelled his entire European programme, including the visits to Vienna and Geneva in connection with the Outer Space Conference and the Conference of Non-Nuclear Powers.'

I finished reading the statement, and most correspondents left the room. Powell and I waited in case there were any questions. The Correspondent of Tass, an old hand at the UN, approached me and said harshly: 'Why the hell did you have to read it with such feelings?' I replied: 'Thank you for the compliment.'

In the course of the afternoon, we saw Brian Urquhart. We discussed the developments of the day, and he remarked that in his opinion U Thant's statement was the strongest ever made by a Secretary-General of the United Nations. This was significant, for Urquhart was the only official of the UN Secretariat who had worked under three Secretaries-General – Trygve Lie, Dag Hammarskjöld and U Thant (he subsequently worked too for Kurt Waldheim and Perez de Cuellar).

The Security Council met on the evening of August 21 at the urgent request of the United States and Denmark. The Soviet Union and Hungary vigorously opposed the inclusion of the item on the agenda, but failed to block it since it was a procedural matter. Ambassador George Ball, who succeeded Arther Goldberg as United States representative, blasted the invasion and called it 'naked agression'. The representative of Czechoslovakia quoted protests that had been lodged by the Ambassador of his country in, respectively, the Soviet Union, Bulgaria, Hungary, Poland and East Germany whose military forces had taken part in the 'illegal occupation'.

Throughout the world there was a strong reaction against the invasion. President Tito of Yugoslavia condemned it, and Nicolae Ceausescu, President of Romania, a member of the Warsaw Pact but which had declined to participate in the invasion, deplored it and warned the Soviet Union that the Romanians would resist any similar attempt against their country. Meanwhile Ceausescu dispatched Corneliu Manescu, his Foreign Minister who had been President of the General Assembly for 1967–8, to New York for talks at the United Nations. On his arrival, he rushed, accompanied only by an interpreter, into a conference with U Thant that lasted over an hour. Neither would disclose the substance of their talks. The only reply I was authorised to give at the press briefing was that they had discussed the 'serious situation prevailing in Eastern Europe'. Manescu also met Ambassador George Ball and the President of the Security Council.

The Communist Party leadership in Romania was seriously concerned about a possible Soviet invasion of their country, and Manescu's journey to the United Nations was a signal to Moscow that Bucharest was prepared for the worst. He was still at that point President of the UN General Assembly, and was on the scene ready to call a meeting of the Security Council if the situation should warrant it. Weeks later, when the uproar over the invasion had subsided, I learned from Bogdan Lewandowski, Ambassador of Poland to the UN and later a UN Under Secretary-General, that the fact that Manescu was President of the Assembly, and had made a hurried trip to the United Nations at the height of the Czech crisis, had been factors in dissuading Moscow from invading Romania.

The Security Council met again on August 22. Denmark presented a draft resolution declaring the Soviet invasion a violation of the UN Charter and calling on the Warsaw Pact countries to withdraw their forces from Czechoslovakia. At the same meeting, it was announced that Hajek was on his way to New York to attend the Security Council. The Council continued its session until the early hours of the next day with Ambassador Malik of the Soviet Union making a desperate effort to defend his government's action. When the voting took place, the resolution received ten affirmative votes, but failed to be adopted because of the Soviet veto. The other vote against it was Hungary.

The Czechoslovak Foreign Minister, Hajek, addressed the meeting of the Council on August 24. This scholarly, white-haired minister, who looked more like a university professor, delivered a sober speech, in English. Quietly, without raising his voice, he called the invasion an act 'of force which could not be justified'. He looked at Ambassador Malik and asked for the name or names of the Czechoslovak leaders who had invited the Warsaw Pact to occupy Czechoslovakia. Malik looked away and did not answer.

Meanwhile, dramatic developments took place in Prague. Soviet troops arrested Alexander Dubček and members of his government. I learned from a Czech friend close to Hajek that when Ludwig Svoboda, President of Czechoslovakia and a holder of the Hero of the Soviet Union decoration, heard this news, he threatened to commit suicide and cancel his visit to Moscow for negotiations with the Kremlin leaders. Dubček and his colleagues were immediately released and allowed to join the Czechoslovak delegation in Moscow.

On August 26, Hajek told U Thant that he had received instructions from his President advising that the negotiations in Moscow were reaching a delicate phase, and it would be helpful if the Security Council were to cease its consideration of the invasion. U Thant suggested that the best way to announce this decision would be in the form of a press release to be issued by the Czechoslovak mission to the UN. Hajek agreed to avoid making another statement that would contradict what he had already said in the Council.

The item of Czechoslovakia remained on the agenda of the Security Council as a matter of record. No action was taken because a permanent member (the Soviet Union) exercised its veto. Eventually, bilateral talks between Prague and Moscow resulted in a return of normal relations between the two countries. But the policy of liberalisation in Eastern Europe received a major setback.

U THANT AND PEKING

U Thant believed in the universality of the United Nations. He thought the exclusion of the People's Republic of China, embracing one fourth of the human race, and a country which under a previous regime, had been a founding member of the UN, unjustified and inexcusable. But he was careful to observe the rules. For it was the Government of the island of Taiwan (Formosa), calling itself the 'Republic of China', which continued, with the support of the United States, to represent China in the United Nations up till 1971.

At his first press conference, as Acting Secretary-General, on December 1, 1961, U Thant was asked if he had any comment on the question of Chinese representation. He replied: 'On such issues I think it would be proper to bear in mind two U Thants. U Thant, the permanent representative of his country, and U Thant as Acting Secretary-General. Of course, U Thant in his first role had certain ideas regarding not only this question but other questions too, and U Thant in his second role is not supposed to express any definitive views on any item apart from the implementation of United Nations resolutions. . . .'

On September 12, 1963, at a press conference in New York, he was asked for his comments on the universality of membership of the United Nations particularly with reference to the People's Republic of China. He replied: 'Universality is a principle which is implied in the Charter itself and a principle to which I fully subscribe. I still maintain this position. I believe in the desirability of universality of membership in the United Nations.'

At another press conference, this time on January 21, 1964, asked to comment on the impending recognition of the People's Republic of China by General de Gaulle, U Thant said: 'It is very difficult and certainly very delicate to assess the foreign policies or attitudes of member–states. It is particularly so when someone in my position has to assess the attitude of a big power, such as France, whose foreign policies and motivations are almost undergoing a revolution, if I may say so I am sure you will understand my reluctance to pass any comment on the prospective decision of the government of France on this matter.'

He continued: 'All I want to say at the moment is that it is difficult to know the true facts about China. News from China, or news about China, generates such intense emotions everywhere that it is difficult if not impossible to discuss this subject rationally and objectively in many parts of the world. I think our attitudes are primarily the result of mass media, as I have stated on previous occasions.

'Our attitudes towards China, or towards any other subject, are the result of what newspapers we read, what radio stations we listen to and also, I think, what part of the world we live in. For instance, an average citizen of the United Kingdom will have a different attitude towards China from that which is held by an average citizen of this country [the United States].'

Continuing his elaborate reply, he made one unusual remark: 'Without attempting to pass any judgement on China, I just want to invite your attention to a remarkably comprehensive, informative and objective book. It is *The Other Side of the River* by Edgar Snow, whom I consider a great authority on China.' It was most unusual for the Secretary-General of the UN to make publicity for a commercial book, regardless of its author. But it was typical of the man to make that statement. He knew Snow and was fond of him, and he had read the book and liked it.

After each press conference, I was in the habit of giving U Thant feedback on the coverage by the major news agencies and newspapers of the various items he had dealt with. When I said that the consensus among the correspondents was that the Secretary-General had given Edgar Snow's book publicity worth several thousands of dollars, he just smiled and said: 'I am glad – Snow is a good man who wrote a great book.'

The year 1971 was the turning-point. In the summer came the announcement from Washington that shook the world: President Richard Nixon of the United States would visit the People's Republic of

China on February 21-28, 1972, ending a period of hostile relations that had extended over twenty years. It was an unpredictable and unexpected diplomatic coup conceived by Nixon's Secretary of State, Henry Kissinger, to stun Moscow and its allies, while the peace negotiations between the United States and the Hanoi government in Vietnam were going through a crucial phase in Paris.

Encouraged by this development, U Thant went further in advocating the seating of Peking in the United Nations. In his introduction to the Report on the Work of the Organisation, covering the period of June 16, 1970, to June 15, 1971, released on September 19, 1971, he stated:

'At a time when the participation of the People's Republic of China in the United Nations seems to be within reach, I very much hope that no more time will be lost in sterile debate on this question and by the use of legalistic arguments to conceal political realities. Although the nature of the solution depends on member-states, it has always been my firm conviction that our Organisation would have undoubtedly been more efficient had it not kept the door closed to one of the largest nations in the world and to those states which – precisely because they were divided and belonged to opposing ideological systems – needed to participate in the United Nations, where they could have found a common ground for working together to overcome their differences.

'The participation of the People's Republic of China will no doubt increase the United Nations' capability of working for the objectives of the Charter. It will also bring closer to realisation the goal of universality of membership of the United Nations, which has been one of my cherished personal aspirations during the last ten years. In this regard, I feel strongly that the admission of the divided countries to the United Nations should not be linked to the solution of the problems resulting from their division. Their accession to membership should, on the contrary, be considered as likely to facilitate the search for solutions to these problems.'

During the twenty-sixth regular session of the General Assembly in 1971, Nixon's forthcoming visit to China overshadowed all other issues. At every previous session, the United States had opposed the seating of mainland China, and argued forcefully that the relevant resolution was one of substance and not procedure, thus requiring a two-thirds majority. This time, in 1971, most delegations believed that, for the sake of consistency, Washington would maintain the same opposition but without the usual vigour and arm-twisting that they had employed in the past. But they were mistaken.

Primarily to appease the strong (Taiwan) China lobby in the US Congress and partly also to make the point that recognition of China, which was to follow the Nixon visit, did not mean abandoning Taiwan, the US delegation to the General Assembly worked hard to block the seating of the Peking delegation in the United Nations and the expulsion of Taiwan. The fact that delegates unfriendly to the United States called this attitude hypocritical did not change the picture.

Twenty-three countries, mostly from Asia and Africa, and led by Albania, Tanzania and Yugoslavia, co-sponsored a draft resolution which was submitted to the Assembly. Significantly the only member of the Warsaw Pact among the sponsors was Romania: this was because of the strained relations between Moscow and Peking.

The draft resolution read:

'The General Assembly recalling the principles of the Charter of the United Nations – considering that the restoration of the lawful rights of the People's Republic of China is essential both for the protection of the Charter of the United Nations and for the cause that the United Nations must serve under the Charter – recognising that the representatives of the Government of the People's Republic of China are the only lawful representatives of China to the United Nations and that the People's Republic of China is one of the five permanent members of the Security Council,

'Decides to restore all its rights to the People's Republic of China and to recognise the representatives of its government as the only legitimate representatives of China to the United Nations, and to expel forthwith the representatives of Chiang Kai-shek from the place which they unlawfully occupy at the United Nations and in all organisations related to it.'*

The General Assembly voted late in the evening of October 25, 1971, and the result of the vote was: 76 in favour, 35 against and 17 abstentions. The vote was conducted by roll call, and when the President of the Assembly announced that the resolution was adopted, there was prolonged applause and some cheering.

Ambassador Salem Selim of Tanzania, overcome with joy, broke into an African dance which lasted a couple of minutes and was shown on US television. Members of the American delegation were outraged, and resented Selim's manifestation of pleasure over their defeat. Ten years later, in December 1981, Salem Selim, then Foreign Minister of

---

*General Assembly records – meeting no. 1976 of October 25, 1971.

Tanzania, was the candidate of the African Group for the post of Secretary-General of the United Nations against Kurt Waldheim. On that occasion the Security Council met in camera and held eighteen ballots, and Selim was vetoed each time. It was the United States that vetoed him, and veteran observers and correspondents recalled his dance after the vote on China ten years earlier.

After the lapse of years, it is interesting to recall the voting that evening on the seating of the People's Republic of China in the UN. Those in favour of the resolution were Afghanistan, Albania, Algeria, Austria, Belgium, Bhutan, Botswana, Bulgaria, Burma, Burundi, the Byelorussian SSR, Cameroon, Canada, Ceylon, Chile, Congo, Cuba, Czechoslovakia, Denmark, Ecuador, Egypt, Equatorial Guinea, Ethiopia, Finland, France, Ghana, Guinea, Guyana, Hungary, Iceland, India, Iran, Iraq, Ireland, Israel, Italy, Kenya, Kuwait, Laos, Libya, Malaysia, Mali, Mauritania, Mexico, Mongolia, Morocco, Nepal, the Netherlands, Nigeria, Norway, Pakistan, the People's Democratic Republic of Yemen, Peru, Poland, Portugal, Romania, Rwanda, Senegal, Sierra Leone, Singapore, Somalia, Sudan, Sweden, Syria, Togo, Trinidad and Tobago, Tunisia, Turkey, Uganda, the Ukrainian SSR, the Soviet Union, the United Kingdom, Tanzania, Yemen, Yugoslavia and Zambia.

Against the resolution were Australia, Bolivia, Brazil, the Central African Republic, Chad, Costa Rica, Dahomey, the Dominican Republic, El Salvador, Gabon, the Gambia, Guatemala, Haiti, Honduras, Ivory Coast, Japan, the Khmer Republic, Lesotho, Liberia, Madagascar, Malawi, Malta, New Zealand, Nicaragua, Niger, Paraguay, the Philippines, Saudi Arabia, South Africa, Swaziland, the United States, Upper Volta, Uruguay, Venezuela and Zaire.

Abstaining were Argentina, Bahrain, Barbados, Colombia, Cyprus, Fiji, Greece, Indonesia, Jamaica, Jordan, Lebanon, Luxembourg, Mauritius, Panama, Qatar, Spain and Thailand.

Overnight, U Thant pondered what he should say about this important event. He thought of addressing the General Assembly, but ruled it out for fear that some militant delegates might start another demonstration against the United States. He was only nine weeks from his retirement, due to take place on December 31, 1971, and planned to stay on in New York to write his memoirs. After several hours, he opted to put his thoughts and views in a carefully-worded statement to be issued as a press release. He gave me the statement on October 26, to be issued and distributed.

It stated: 'The United Nations has been confronted for over twenty years with the problem of the participation of the People's Republic of China. Over the years the representatives of nearly every country in the world have on many occasions expressed the positions, the hopes and also the misgivings of their governments concerning the solution to this fundamental problem. The debate which we have witnessed during the last ten days has shown very clearly that the issue is one which still involves deep emotions and strong convictions. As Secretary-General of the United Nations, I have always advocated the participation of the People's Republic of China in the work of this Organisation, but I have also always respected as I still do, the opinion of every member–state, even when I personally do not agree with it.

'Now that the Assembly has taken a decision that the question has been settled, let us not lose time and energy by falling into the tempta-tion of judging attitudes which now belong to the past, of awakening suspicions which have already been overcome. Let us unanimously and resolutely engage on the new road which opens today before us. I solemnly appeal to all member–states to leave no room for bitterness, but on the contrary to abide by the decision of the General Assembly and endorse the tremendous step forward which has been taken last night.

'I strongly believe that the presence amongst us of the People's Republic of China, which is now to become a reality, attests to the con-siderable improvement in the international situation, and will eventually lead to the strengthening and betterment of the Organisation. I have always said that room should be made in the United Nations for member–governments with widely differing economic and social systems. Now, at the close of this debate, it seems that the Organisation will fulfil more fully one of the basic purposes of the Charter, "to be a centre for harmonising the actions of nations". Whatever their sentiment as to the desirable outcome of the debate, I think almost all member–states agreed that the absence of the People's Republic of China from the Organisation gave it a certain artificiality, and adversely affected its authority. The decision reached last night may enable us to solve more effectively the inter-national problems with which we are confronted. However, this will imply that no member turns its back on the new tasks and new prospects which are now facing the international community.

'It is indeed necessary for our Organisation to reflect the changes which occur in the international arena. We have been gratified to see new trends towards détente and co-operation. The bold decision made by the President of the United States to visit the People's Republic of China, thereby overlooking two decades of hostility, is one of the positive and hopeful developments which we have watched recently. Also, the readiness of the government of the People's Republic of China to overcome long-standing fears and suspicions and to accept this dialogue gives us a clear image of its maturity and constructiveness.

'It is my hope that last night's decision by the General Assembly will be considered in the light of all these developments, and that the true statesmanship already displayed by the leaders of both sides will once again be reflected in their continued acceptance of the goals of the United Nations.

'I feel sad at the departure of the members of the Permanent Mission of "the Republic of China" from the halls of the United Nations. My personal relations with its Permanent Representative and his colleagues for the past ten years have been very warm, and I have always held Ambassador Liu Chieh in high esteem for his great human qualities. However, the international community through its forum has pronounced its decision, and it has to be respected.

'The recognition of the new role that the People's Republic of China is now playing in international life has been expressed by the ever-growing number of member–states who have normalised their relations with that country.

'Last night's vote should not be considered in terms of either victory or defeat, but as an essential step towards a more effective and realistic international system. The twenty-sixth session of the General Assembly will thus have been a session of decision.'*

Four days later, on October 30, U Thant was rushed to Le Roy Hospital in New York City with a bleeding ulcer.

A large Chinese delegation headed by Chiao Kuan-Hua, deputy Minister of Foreign Affairs, and Huang Hua, formerly Ambassador to Ottawa, now arrived in New York. Edgar Snow appeared at the same time, and it soon became evident he was acting as adviser to the Chinese.

On November 12, Snow came to see me at my office. At first he enquired about U Thant's health and asked whether he was receiving visitors at the hospital. When I replied in the affirmative, Snow said that Chiao Kuan-Hua and Huang Hua wanted to visit U Thant to present their credentials to him personally. It was clear he came to me so that I would send this request directly to the Secretary-General without going through the normal channels. That would have been Sinan Korle, Chief

---

*Press release SG/SM/1565 issued on 26 October 1971.

of Protocol, who in turn would report to Narasimhan (India), *Chef de Cabinet*, in the Secretary-General's absence.

Relations between China and India were strained, and it was obvious that the Chinese did not wish to go to an Indian official of the UN Secretariat to reach U Thant. They were keen on dealing with the Secretary-General in person. I called Don Thomas who, for security reasons, had a room next to the Secretary-General at the hospital. I gave him the message, requesting him to pass it on and let me know the answer. Then I called Korle and Narasimhan to inform them of what I had done. Korle protested, insisting that presentation of credentials never took place in a hospital room, but I reminded him of the unusual circumstances and in any event it was up to the Secretary-General to decide. There was no comment from Narasimhan. An hour later, Thomas was on the phone to say that U Thant would be happy to receive the Chinese at 11.00 a.m. on Saturday, November 14. I passed this information on to Snow, Korle and Narasimhan.

I arrived at the hospital at 10.30 on November 14, to find that there were ten correspondents including two TV cameras waiting at the door. I spoke to them indicating they were free to film the arrival and departure of the delegates, but no cameras could be allowed inside U Thant's room. I promised to brief them after the event. They agreed.

The Chief of Protocol received the two Chinese delegates and a woman interpreter at the door of the hospital and escorted them to U Thant's room on the second floor. Just inside the door, a pale but beaming U Thant, wearing a blue dressing-gown, warmly greeted his guests. They engaged, through the interpreter, in small talk about the weather in New York and Peking and Chinese food.

U Thant recalled his visit to Peking with U Nu in 1954, and his meeting with Premier Chou En-lai. Chiao Kuan-hua gave him two sets of credentials, one for himself as chairman of the delegation, and the second for Huang Hua as permanent representative of China to the UN. His words, through the interpreter, were: 'The delegation of China does this with respect and honour for U Thant.' The whole exercise was, in some way, an expression of China's appreciation for the numerous statements by U Thant, advocating the seating of the People's Republic in the UN.

Following the presentation, I gave the waiting reporters an account of what had happened. The four-minute briefing was filmed and used, *in toto*, on the 7 o'clock news bulletins of two networks, NBC and CBS.

China or 'Red China', as the American information media insisted on calling it – was very much in the news those days.

THE FINANCIAL PROBLEM

U Thant inherited the financial problem of the UN. It began with the establishment of UNEF, the UN peacekeeping force for the Middle East in 1956, after the tripartite invasion of Suez. By 1957–8 more than thirty countries, mainly members of the Soviet Bloc, and several Arab states refused to pay their share of the costs, claiming that the governments responsible (Britain, France and Israel) should foot the entire bill. By the end of 1960, there was a deficit of some $86.9 million in the costs of UNEF and the UN force in the Congo.

One of U Thant's first major initiatives as Acting Secretary-General was a proposal for a $200 million bond issue to ease the Organisation's finances. The draft resolution to the General Assembly was sponsored by Canada, Denmark, Ethiopia, the Federation of Malaya, the Netherlands, Norway, Pakistan, Tunisia and Yugoslavia. It did not identify the plan as U Thant's, but he himself acknowledged that he had participated in its formation.

The idea was originally advanced by the United States, but U Thant accepted it and became its sponsor in private consultations, which he began a few days after his appointment. The details were worked out by the UN Comptroller, Bruce Turner, and U Thant himself. The resolution was submitted to the Fifth Committee on December 16, 1961, and the vote was 58 to 13 with 28 abstaining. Both the Soviet Union and France voted against it. The sale of bonds relieved the financial pressure for the moment, but the response to the plan was disappointing. Only sixty-five states, including five non-members, made purchases. The United States bought half of the total and eventually purchases of bonds reached $154.7 million.

On July 20, 1962, the International Court of Justice delivered, as requested by the General Assembly, an advisory opinion to the effect that 'expenses of the Organisation' meant all expenses approved by the General Assembly.

In 1964, the United States spearheaded a move in the General Assembly to apply article 17 of the UN Charter – 'that the expenses of the Organisation shall be borne by all members' and article 19 – 'A member falling in arrears by two years must be deprived of its vote in the General Assembly.'

By that time, the United Nations was in debt to the tune of $134 million despite the bond issue. Even meeting the payroll of the staff was in doubt. Meanwhile, the Soviet Union was adamant in refusing to yield to pressure. The opening of the nineteenth Assembly was postponed from September till December.

Finally, on the eve of the opening, agreement was reached between the United States, the Soviet Union, France and Britain on a formula to allow the Assembly to transact essential and non-controversial business by unanimous consent, without taking a formal vote.

When the General Assembly reconvened on January 18, 1965, the confrontation between the United States and the Soviet Union was averted when Ambassador Adlai Stevenson declared that in order to prevent the will of the majority from 'being frustrated by one member', the United States would not invoke Article 19. During the regular session in 1965, a consensus emerged that there should be voluntary contributions by member–states with the highly-developed countries paying the larger sums. U Thant seized on this and issued an urgent appeal to all members to make voluntary contributions. The United Kingdom announced a contribution of $10 million dollars. Both the Soviet Union and France agreed to make contributions without prejudice to their stated positions. Nevertheless, when U Thant retired on December 31, 1971, unpaid regular budget assessments were in excess of $65 million in addition to more than $50 million in debts incurred for past and continuing peacekeeping operations.

THE UNITED NATIONS UNIVERSITY

In 1969, U Thant, the former teacher, proposed the creation of an international university to serve a world increasingly preoccupied with problems beyond the borders of any individual country. His proposal came towards the end of the introduction to the Secretary-General's annual report to the twenty-fourth session of the General Assembly.

He stated: 'I feel that the time has come when serious thought may be given to the establishment of a United Nations university, truly international in character, and devoted to the Charter objectives of peace and progress.' He suggested that the UN Education, Scientific and Cultural Organisation (UNESCO) should develop the proposal, which would bring together students and teachers from many nations. 'Even in their formative years they would be able to break down the barriers between nations and cultures which create only misunderstandings and mistrust,' he said.

In 1970, ECOSOC invited the General Conference of UNESCO to submit its opinion on the proposal to the twenty-fifth session of the General Assembly. Introducing the item to the Second Committee of the General Assembly in 1971, U Thant stated: 'This is a proposal in which I have taken a great personal interest. When I suggested to the Assembly that serious thought be given to such a proposal, it was in the context of the darkening situation for the maintenance of international peace and security. The primary objective of the proposed university was to promote international understanding. I felt strongly that such an institution would radiate a beneficial influence throughout the world, especially among the rising generation, and would help to break down moral and intellectual barriers between nations. This remains my firm belief.'

In September 1971, the UNESCO Feasibility Study was completed, and the report of the UN Panel of Experts was presented to U Thant in November, six weeks before he was due to retire.

During that period, correspondents and delegates alike suggested that the main reason why U Thant was pushing hard for the establishment of the UN University was that he wanted to be named its first Rector. When I brought those rumours to his attention, he smiled and said: 'Let them speculate.' Somehow, it did not seem to bother him to know that his background as a teacher and his impending retirement were being linked in the context of the proposal for a UN University.

In 1972, the General Conference of UNESCO adopted a resolution recommending to the UN General Assembly the creation of an international university and the establishment of a Founding Committee. On December 11, 1972, the General Assembly approved the establishment of a United Nations University (UNU).

In June 1973, the Government of Japan pledged $100 million (US dollars) to UNU, and offered it headquarters facilities in Tokyo. Ironically, 1974 was the year that witnessed the appointment of the members of the Council of the University and it was in November, the month in which U Thant died, that James M. Hester from the United States was appointed first Rector of UNU. In December, the University started functioning with temporary offices in the Imperial Hotel, Tokyo. In January 1975, the Council met for the first time in Tokyo and approved three initial priority areas: World Hunger; Human and Social Development; and the Use and Management of Natural Resources.

In 1980, the Council reported to the United Nations General Assembly and the Executive Board of UNESCO that the UNU was operating nineteen networks, twenty-six associated institutions and over 100 research and training units located in more than sixty countries. It awarded 225 fellowships and produced 140 publications. On September 1 that year, Soedjatmoko, an Indonesian scholar, assumed his duties as the second Rector of UNU. The current Rector is Hector Gurgulino de Souza from Brazil.

Thus an idea conceived by the only Asian to occupy the post of UN Secretary-General, and a Buddhist, became a reality in a leading Asian-Buddhist country. It is sad that he did not live long enough to see his dream fulfilled.

8

U THANT'S DEPARTURE

U Thant's tenth and last year in office, 1971, was a particularly difficult one for him. To delegates who approached him, proposing that he should accept a third term, he quipped that he was already suffering from the law of 'diminishing returns', and that no Secretary-General should accept more than a single term of five years – he had now served two terms totalling ten years.

His health was failing, and the sudden eruption of his ulcer in late October had kept him away from his office for five weeks. After his discharge from hospital on November 27, he went to his residence at Riverdale for a rest. But the pressure of work continued and he was compelled to carry out several tasks during the time when he should have been convalescing. After nine days at home, he returned to his office on December 6 to face a multitude of problems. Fighting between West Pakistan and India had started on December 3. India announced its recognition of the former East Pakistan as the Republic of Bangladesh on December 6.

He felt saddened over the loss of life and destruction in the Indian sub-continent and the plight of tens of thousands of refugees from East Pakistan. On December 9, Ralph Bunche, one of U Thant's close associates, died in hospital after a long illness. The same day, U Thant asked me to announce his decision to cancel the Human Rights Day concert scheduled for the next day, December 10. In explanation I said: 'This decision was taken in the light of the present international situation and the pressure of work on the principal organs of the UN.' The General Assembly was in session and its committees were meeting day and night to finish their work by December 21.

As if to add to the problems facing U Thant, A. Hamid (from Pakistan), the head of the Office of Public Information, recommended the withdrawal of the UN press accreditations from two Chinese correspondents from Taiwan, T.C. Tang and C.C. Lin, representing the 'Central China News Agency'. The proposal was legally sound in view of the decision of the General Assembly to expel the Government of Formosa from the UN and to seat Peking, but the abrupt and high-handed action taken by the UN Secretariat in closing the offices and barring the two correspondents entry into the building was clumsy and unnecessary. I was against it and voiced my opinion. U Thant was always popular with the correspondents, and I failed to see why, only twelve days before his retirement, he should take an action they would resent. To my disappointment, after consulting Stavropoulos (Greece), his legal counsel, he elected to go along with Hamid's advice and bar the two journalists. On December 17, 1971, the entire daily press briefing, which lasted more than 45 minutes, was taken up with this problem, with William Powell and myself faced by angry correspondents, defending the withdrawal of UN accreditations from the two Chinese Nationalists.

Meanwhile, candidates for the post of Secretary-General were coming forward. Among the front-runners were Max Jakobson of Finland, Kurt Waldheim of Austria and Prince Sadruddin Agha Khan, to which press reports added half a dozen others from every corner of the globe. On December 21, 1971, the Security Council met in camera, and elected Kurt Waldheim Secretary-General to succeed U Thant, and the General Assembly confirmed the appointment.

Four weeks earlier, I had said to U Thant that in view of his imminent departure I thought it better, for my own part to leave UN Head-quarters in New York and seek, with his blessings, a position with the United Nations Office at Geneva. Reluctantly he agreed to release me ten days before his retirement.

Kurt Waldheim assumed his new post as the fourth Secretary-General on January 1, 1972. U Thant was keen to stay on for a little while at Riverdale, New York, in his comfortable fourteen-room house, with a large garden and a swimming pool. There he lived with his wife, Daw Thien Tin, his daughter Aye Aye, his son-in-law Tyn Myint U, and his grandchildren. Waldheim wanted to live in Manhattan and agreed that U Thant could stay as long as he wanted at Riverdale.

Six months later, U Thant bought a magnificent mansion in Harrison, a small picturesque town in upstate New York. He had received a large lump sum from the United Nations, and another from his publisher as a royalty advance for his memoirs.

I kept in touch with him by correspondence. In September 1972, he wrote me a cheerful letter announcing his complete recovery. In October 1973, I visited him at his new home, and we had a long chat. He served tea and Burmese cookies and took pride in showing me around. A private swimming pool was being built, for swimming was his greatest passion. A new black Cadillac was in the garage. He introduced me to John, his driver, a retired UN security guard.

U Thant was living in style and I was happy to see it because I felt he had earned it. He spoke at length about his memoirs to which he was putting the finishing touches. I asked about his health and he said he was fine except for a swelling in his mouth. The doctors had taken X-rays and tests, and he was waiting for the results. He asked John to drive me to the station to take a train back to New York City.

When I said good-bye, I did not realise that it was the last time I would ever see him. On November 11, 1973, he was operated on for cancer of the larynx at the Harkness Pavilion of Columbia Presbyterian Medical Center, and was allowed to go home three weeks later.

In October 1974, I was back in New York on a mission for UNCTAD, and as I had heard that U Thant was ill again, I called his home hoping to talk to his daughter, Aye Aye, and enquire about his health. To my surprise, he answered the phone himself. His voice was weak and I sensed that he spoke with difficulty.

I asked if I could see him. I remember him replying; 'I am sorry I can't see you, I am not seeing anybody these days. You will understand, Ramses.'

Those were his last words to me.

On November 21, he was readmitted to the Harkness Pavilion, and four days later, on November 25, he died. He was sixty-five years old. May he rest in peace.

Although, both in his capacity as Secretary-General of the United Nations and in his personal character, U Thant had been a conciliator, he became in death a symbol of the deep political divisions in his own country. Because he had been an ally of the former Premier U Nu, deposed in 1962, the government of Ne Win planned only the minimum of ceremonial when the body was returned to Rangoon on November 30, five days after his death. The public was barred from the airport, and although his family had sought to have him interred near Rangoon's holiest shrine, the Shwe Dagon pagoda, the burial was scheduled to take place instead at a public cemetery.

On December 1, just as the official funeral procession was about to set off, some 20,000 students and Buddhist monks seized U Thant's body and drove it off in a truck to Rangoon University. The government thereupon closed all universities and secondary schools, but the body continued to lie in state at the University watched over by militant students. The police stormed the campus and, having retrieved the body, took it to the family's mausoleum near Shwe Dagon. Angered and inflamed, the students set fire to public buildings, and street riots broke out. The government proclaimed martial law, and troops and police arrested thousands of demonstrators. U Thant's body was finally sealed by the authorities in a tomb near the Pagoda.

It was a tragic thing to happen to the remains of a man who had loved humanity and abhorred violence throughout his life.

9

SUMMING-UP

In drafting the United Nations Charter at San Francisco in 1945, the founding fathers resolved that the Secretary-General should be an eminent person from a small neutral country. Citizens of permanent members of the Security Council, or middle powers such as India or Brazil, were excluded. That understanding has since become a tradition.

The first Secretary-General was Norway's Trygve Lie (1946–53), followed by Sweden's Dag Hammarskjöld (1953–61), Burma's U Thant (1961–71), Austria's Kurt Waldheim (1971–81), and Peru's Javier Perez de Cuellar, whose second term is due to end in 1991. At the time of writing, the last-named has become the oldest serving Secretary-General.

Article 97 of the UN Charter states: 'The Secretary-General shall be appointed by the General Assembly upon the recommendation of the Security Council.' The Council's role is crucial since the five permanent members (China, France, Britain, the United States and the Soviet Union) can exercise the right of veto. No Secretary-General can be appointed against the wish of any of them.

In December 1981, the Security Council met eighteen times to elect a new Secretary-General. Kurt Waldheim wanted a third term, and against him ran Salem Selim, Foreign Minister of Tanzania. Both of them were vetoed at each one of the eighteen meetings. It was later learned that Selim had been vetoed by the United States and Waldheim by China. In a roundabout way, China revealed that its veto had not been personal: 'Mr Waldheim had enough honour in serving two terms totalling ten years,' was the message conveyed. It was during that impasse that Perez de Cuellar's name was proposed, and he was elected as the fifth Secretary-General, also the first from Latin America.

United States influence has always been evident in the UN Secretariat. The proximity of New York to Washington, and even the physical location of the US Mission across First Avenue, some 100 metres away from UN Headquarters, have contributed to that influence. In 1986, when Perez de Cuellar's first term ended, General Vernon Walters, the United States Ambassador to the United Nations, orchestrated the Secretary-General's re-election. General Walters persuaded the Chinese not to use their veto; it was no secret that they had favoured an African candidate.

Article 99 confers upon the Secretary-General an important political task: 'The Secretary-General may bring to the attention of the Security Council any matter which, in his opinion, may threaten the maintenance of international peace and security.'

In June 1950, when North Korea invaded the South, Trygve Lie invoked Article 99 and called an emergency meeting of the Security Council. The Soviet Ambassador Jacob Malik happened to be absent, boycotting the Council in protest at the presence of Taiwan (i.e. Nationalist China). That absence enabled the Council to adopt a resolution setting up a UN Command under the leadership of the United States to stem the aggression from the North. Lie's initiative angered the Russians, and when he ran for re-election in 1951, the Soviet Union vetoed him. The United States, however, succeeded in having the General Assembly extend his mandate for two years. The Soviets declared that procedure illegal and boycotted Lie; and he, realising the futility of continuing in office under such circumstances, resigned.

In July 1953, after a frantic search for a successor, the Security Council, on the recommendation of France, elected Dag Hammarskjöld, a Swedish economist. Hammarskjöld brought to the office of the Secretary-General his own style of quiet diplomacy, plus an articulate definition of the international civil servant: 'He should respond to the General Assembly or to the Security Council, even if it means taking a political stand. . . .'

For Hammarskjöld, the UN Charter was sacrosanct. When Britain, France and Israel invaded Suez in 1956 in retaliation for the nationalisation by President Nasser of the Suez Canal Company, Hammarskjöld declared in an emergency Security Council meeting, called by the United States: 'The principles of the Charter are holier than the policies of any single nation or people.' He further stated that if any country did not agree with his position, he would resign.

At the time, those who did not like Hammarskjöld – they were not many – argued that the United States, which strongly opposed the Suez invasion, encouraged him. True, President Eisenhower, together with Secretary of State John Foster Dulles, went as far as to threaten sanctions against the countries which had mounted the invasion. Nevertheless, Hammarskjöld manifested personal courage in speaking up against two permanent members of the Security Council – Britain and France – and Israel, their ally in the Suez adventure.

Following a cease-fire on the Suez front, Lester Pearson, Prime Minister of Canada, proposed in the General Assembly – convened in an emergency session after two vetoes in the Security Council – the creation of a United Nations Emergency Force (UNEF) to allow the withdrawal of British, French and Israeli forces from Port Said, Sinai and the Gaza strip.

Hammarskjöld, with the able assistance of a small staff headed by Ralph Bunche and Brian Urquhart, worked day and night to put a force together in record time. Hammarskjöld flew to Egypt to see President Nasser. In a marathon meeting lasting seven hours at a rest-house near Cairo, Nasser agreed to the stationing of UNEF on Egyptian territory. Originally UNEF was to be positioned on both sides of the armistice lines (Egypt and Israel), but Israel refused.

In 1960, Hammarskjöld invoked Article 99 of the Charter in response to an appeal from Patrice Lumumba, Prime Minister of the Congo, and the Security Council authorised the Secretary-General to dispatch a UN force to Belgium's former colony. In the Congo, Hammarskjöld expanded the role of both the Secretary-General and of UN peacekeeping to such an extent that he had become virtually *persona non grata* to the Soviet Union. This culminated in Khrushchev's demand in the General Assembly that Hammarskjöld be replaced by a *troika*. As had already been shown in the case of Trygve Lie, it was difficult for a Secretary-General, boycotted by one of the superpowers, to function. Hammarskjöld's tragic and untimely death while on a peace mission in September 1961 saved him from resigning under Soviet pressure.

U Thant, too, was a compromise candidate, and it was partly in order to defeat the *troika* that the United States took a leading part in his election. The Burmese diplomat, a leading figure in the emerging Afro–Asian Group, was a candidate whom the Soviets could not veto. Appointed at first for one year as Acting Secretary-General, in November 1961, he was confirmed for a full term in November 1962. His confirmation followed his dramatic intervention in the Cuban missile crisis, which enabled Khrushchev to back down by agreeing to dismantle and remove the Soviet missiles from Cuba.

That development was most significant. The Soviet Union, after boycotting Trygve Lie over his role in Korea and forcing him to resign, and then turning against Hammarskjöld because of his role in the Congo, had renewed its confidence in the Secretary-General's office through the person of U Thant. Throughout the Cuban Crisis, Khrushchev's messages were addressed 'Dear U Thant'.

U Thant had met Khrushchev during an official visit to the Soviet Union as Acting Secretary-General, in the summer of 1962. The Soviet leader was at his summer dacha in Yalta by the Black Sea. U Thant and his party flew there from Moscow, and had lunch with Khrushchev and his family followed by a long *tête-à-tête* talk between the two of them with only an interpreter in attendance. Later, Khrushchev invited U Thant to join him in a swim in the Black Sea.

U Thant had good relations with the United States. He was a close friend of Ambassador Adlai Stevenson, who had helped to promote his candidacy in 1961. He was also friendly with Sir Patrick Dean, the British Ambassador to the UN. It was Sir Patrick who arranged U Thant's official visit to the United Kingdom in 1962. Although (or perhaps because) he was deeply religious, U Thant was tolerant and abhorred fanaticism. He harboured no ill-feeling towards the former colonial power which had ruled his native Burma. His visit to London was a success: he hit it off well with Prime Minister Macmillan and Foreign Secretary Lord Home, and had a moving personal audience with Queen Elizabeth.

Hammarskjöld and U Thant came from two different worlds. One, a Swedish aristocrat, was reserved and aloof; the other was modest, down-to-earth, outspoken. Those who knew them well dubbed Hammarskjöld the 'Eastern mystic' and characterised U Thant as 'direct, almost Western'. Yet they had much in common. Both were activists; impartial, but not neutral. Both lived comfortably but simply and without fanfare – Hammarskjöld alone in a pleasant apartment on Manhattan's East Side; U Thant with his wife, daughter, son-in-law and grandchildren in a large house at Riverdale. The uninformed public may have thought U Thant a rather dull choice, and a typical compromise, after the dynamic and intellectually brilliant Hammarskjöld. As they got the full measure of U Thant with the journey of time, this unfavourable comparison was forgotten.

As Secretary-General, each had a small cabinet. Hammarskjöld elected to rely on an assistant personally chosen from the Swedish Foreign Office, as well as Andrew Cordier (United States) who was Executive Assistant – replaced by C.V. Narasimhan (India) as *Chef de Cabinet* in 1961, only a few weeks before his fateful trip to the Congo. U Thant inherited Narasimhan and gave him *carte blanche* in the administrative running of the Secretariat.

Hammarskjöld was reserved in his press relations. In a strange way, he was shy of publicity and feared that inquisitive reporters would disrupt his quiet diplomacy. U Thant was exactly the opposite. He liked the press, was open (perhaps too open) with correspondents and took them into his confidence.

The honeymoon lasted till May 1967. When U Thant, on the advice of Ralph Bunche, complied with Nasser's request to withdraw UNEF from Sinai and Gaza without referring the crisis to the Security Council, press reaction was savage. From a purely legal point of view, U Thant was right, since UNEF was stationed on Egyptian territory with Egypt's consent. But the Middle East situation was complex and explosive. Israel used the withdrawal of UNEF and the closure of the Straits of Tiran as a pretext to launch its fateful attack in June 1967.

Kurt Waldheim of Austria and Max Jakobson of Finland, as we have already mentioned, were two leading candidates to succeed U Thant in 1971. I knew Waldheim as Ambassador to the United Nations, and in early December he invited me to a *tête-à-tête* luncheon in the Delegates' dining room. We engaged in small talk, then proceeded to the obvious. Suddenly Waldheim declared that it was time for U Thant to issue a public statement on the succession. Although he did not elaborate, the implication was clear. We were so engrossed in this matter that I neglected to inform Waldheim of my plans to leave New York for a new posting in Geneva.

As a matter of course, I reported to U Thant Waldheim's remarks about a public statement. U Thant's immediate comment was: 'How could I do such a thing? It is up to the Security Council to decide.'

By coincidence, my wife and I left New York for Geneva, on December 21, the very day the Security Council elected Kurt Waldheim Secretary-General. In March 1972, I literally ran into him in the corridors of the Palais des Nations. I stopped to pay my respects. We shook hands. He then publicly rebuked me: 'You have deserted me, Mr Nassif – left me without a spokesman.' I was taken aback and tried to explain, but he cut me short: 'We will talk later.'

I asked for an appointment to see him, but Anton Prohaska, one of his aides, told me it was not necessary. The message was clear: The Secretary-General resented your departure – you should have stayed on the job until he had decided on who should replace you, and then faded away.

I did not join those who denounced Kurt Waldheim over his alleged activities as a *Wehrmacht* officer during the Second World War.

Kurt Waldheim brought a new style to the Office of the Secretary-General, on the thirty-eighth floor of the Glass House on the East River. The whole floor was redecorated, recarpeted and, with few exceptions, restaffed. Procedures and appearances became very important.

The residence was no longer a house at Riverdale but a sumptuous town house in Sutton Place, a very fashionable New York address. It is a beautiful two-storeyed mansion overlooking the East River, on loan to the United Nations for a nominal rent. The United Nations pays for its upkeep and maintenance.

During his ten-year tenure, Waldheim maintained good relations with all the permanent members of the Security Council – the United States, the Soviet Union, Britain, France and China. He chaired the International Peace Conference on the Middle East in Geneva in December 1973, and he made a serious effort to free the American hostages from captivity in Teheran: after convening the Security Council, he flew to the Iranian capital on a mission which was fraught with danger. But the hostages remained in captivity. Waldheim also achieved a measure of success towards ending the communal strife in Cyprus.

I twice met Javier Perez de Cuellar, Waldheim's successor. The first time was in his office on the thirty-eighth floor of UN Headquarters in the summer of 1982. The appointment, which had been arranged by his spokesman François Giuliani, was so that I could interview him for the *Irish Times*. Perez de Cuellar was extremely courteous – and he spoke slowly measuring every word. It was his first year in office, and he was obviously enjoying the job. He went out of his way to say that he liked the press.

The second meeting was during an official visit by the Secretary-General to Ireland in April 1983. In the course of our conversation at his hotel suite, I suggested that he might consider inviting former Presidents of the UN General Assembly to New York to discuss the future of the Organisation. I added that perhaps an idea or two would emerge from such an encounter, which would help the Secretary-General in his difficult task.

He listened carefully, and asked for a note I had prepared with a list of the former Presidents. In May, I received a letter from Perez de Cuellar thanking me for my proposal, but stating that 1983 would not be the best time because he expected to be receiving a large number of heads of state and government following the call of the Non-Aligned Summit in New Delhi.

The Secretary-General's letter was followed by another from Giuliani. He had sent my proposal to Yasuchi Akashi, head of DPI (the Department of Public Information) in connection with the fortieth anniversary of the UN in 1985. The proposal was then referred to

UNITAR (the UN Institute for Training and Research). The encounter of the Presidents did indeed materialise in New York in the summer of 1985. I had indirectly heard of the preparations, so I took the liberty of sending a personal letter to Perez de Cuellar hinting that it might be appropriate for me to attend as an observer. My letter remained unanswered.

Although he comes from Peru, a poor Third World country, it appears that Perez de Cuellar favours the high living of his predecessor; he continues to live in the Sutton Place mansion, which was redecorated at great expense with voluntary contributions raised by the United Nations Association of the United States.

In the Secretary-General's first report to the General Assembly in September 1982, Perez de Cuellar employed blunt language in urging the Security Council to review its provisions for collective security, insisting that all member-states should live up to their obligations under the Charter. But his call went unheeded. Perez de Cuellar came very close to a settlement in Cyprus, but the hardline attitude of President Spyros Kyprianou put a last-minute hurdle in the way of the delicate negotiations.

The Secretary-General is a very cautious man. His personal intervention in the brutal Iraq-Iran war to protect civilians on both sides prevailed for a while. He shunned invoking Article 99 and waited for the Security Council to act, despatching him to Teheran and Baghdad to negotiate the implementation of Resolution 598 for a cease-fire. It was a case of 'mission impossible', but the Secretary-General had no choice but to comply. Unfortunately, he came away empty-handed. As 1988 dawned, the senseless and immensely bloody war continued unabated.

Perhaps it is unfair to blame any one Secretary-General for the decline of the Organisation. The Middle East war of June 1967, after the withdrawal of UNEF, tarnished the image of the United Nations. In the 1970s, multilateralism started losing ground in favour of bilateralism. Leading nations of the Non-Aligned Group, and those of the Group of 77 (membership is almost identical but the origin is different) pay lip-service to the United Nations. In the General Assembly, they are quick to exhort all member-countries, especially the Western ones, to strengthen the world organisation and give teeth to its resolutions. Meanwhile, the same countries enter into long-term bilateral agreements and protocols with the United States, the Soviet Union, Japan, Britain, West Germany or France.

Equally at fault is the attitude of countries from the Third World, sometimes with the support of the Soviet Union and the Socialist countries. They rally to vote in the UN General Assembly for resolutions unacceptable to the West. The so-called automatic majority on political or economic issues has damaged the prestige and credibility of the United Nations.

Even more serious is the tendency of the superpowers in recent years to conduct their serious business outside the United Nations. In 1985, when gigantic preparations were being made in Geneva for the first Reagan-Gorbachev Summit, the UN Secretary-General discreetly offered the premises of the Palais des Nations, but his offer was ignored – the American and Soviet authorities made their own arrangements with the Swiss government. Again, US Secretary of State George Shultz met Soviet Foreign Minister Edward Shevardnadze in Geneva in November 1987. Their negotiations resulted in agreement banning medium- and short-range missiles. The meetings were at the Soviet and United States missions on the Avenue de la Paix. There was no United Nations involvement or link whatever. The historic treaty was signed by President Reagan and General Secretary Gorbachev at the Washington Summit on December 8, 1987.

U Thant was fond of saying: 'The Secretary-General, as well as the Organisation, suffer from the law of diminishing returns. We must remember, the United Nations is a mirror of its members. It shall be as strong or as weak as its members want it to be.'

INDEX